The Backyard Bowyer

Nicholas Tomihama

Levi Dream Publishing

***For my wife Angela,
and Levi, my little arrow.***

"*Like arrows in the hands of a warrior
are sons born in one's youth.
Blessed is the man
whose quiver is full of them.*"
-*Psalms 127 : 4-5*

Table of Contents

Introduction	6
Tools	13
Building a Tiller	19
Tillering Stick	20
Tillering Tree	30
Bow Scale	35
Flat Bow	36
Design	37
Selecting Wood	42
Roughing the Bow	45
Backing the Bow	59
Rough Tillering	64
Tillering	74
Finishing	89
Long Bow	106
Design	107
Selecting Wood	110
Roughing the Bow	111
Tillering	122
Finishing	128
Handle Wrap and Arrow Rest	136
Glossary	150
Acknowledgments	153
Bonus Track	154

Levi Dream Publishing ©2010

ALL RIGHTS RESERVED. No part of this book may be reproduced or transmitted in any form by any means, electronic or mechanical, including photocopying or recording, or by any information storage and retrieval system, except as may be expressly permitted in writing from the publisher. Requests for permission should be addressed to Levi Dream Publishing, Attn: Rights and Permissions, P.O. Box 75203, Honolulu, HI 96836-0203.

Printed in the USA

ISBN 978-0-9832481-0-1

Library of Congress Cataloging-in-Publication Data is available on file.
194 Pages | 341 Pictures | 19514 Words

The Backyard Bowyer

A Little Warning

The big difference between the bows in this book and what I call modern bows is that a wood bow is much more prone to violently breaking than a modern bow. If you are used to shooting a compound or a recurve, these simple wooden bows shoot much differently. They require more babying concerning things most compound and recurve shooters don't have to deal with.

Most modern bow limbs are at least party composed of fiberglass or carbon fiber. These composites are very tough, and as a result they can be drawn farther, be much shorter, and withstand much more abuse than all-wood bows.

All-wood bows need to be warmed up, usually with one or two pulls to half-draw before a shooting session. The wood, which has much less flex and strength than fiberglass, needs time to get used to bending. Your wood bow also needs to be drawn slower than modern bows. Modern bows, especially compounds, are drawn quicker to overcome the quick buildup of early-draw weight. Simple bows don't have any let off, and at full draw, all the bow's weight is on you. Since the bow is at full weight the entire time it is held a full draw, holding it too long could cause it to break over time. A good rule is to aim, draw slowly and then release once fully drawn.

These bows don't have a wall or stop to keep you from pulling the bow too far. The bow itself will give no warning or indication that it is about to fail from being overdrawn, so it is very important to draw to the same length every time. Your bow is just that, your bow. It needs to be built to your draw length, which is personal. As an example, I'm a good inch or so taller than my wife, but her draw is about an inch longer than mine. Not everyone draws based on their height.

If a bow is overdrawn, especially if it is of a higher-weight, there is a good chance it could explode. This can be very dangerous and cause serious injury to you or those around you. Wooden bows also are affected by temperature and humidity, especially high temperatures and low humidity. High humidity may lower your bow's speed and weight, but low humidity could cause your bow to simply snap. It is a bad idea to keep your bow in a hot car for extended periods, though even modern bows can be hurt by this.

Even though simple bows have their drawbacks, they are usually just as effective as most modern bows, and are much simpler to maintain and keep tuned. Especially when you build them yourself, they require great care to bring them past the early stages of their lives. Once they pass this infant stage, wooden bows can be as durable and tough as fiberglass bows, all things considered.

     Building bows is one of the most fulfilling and gratifying things I have personally done. They are truly alive, each one with its own personality. You'll never know exactly what different woods will do, no matter how many bows you build. There will always be a challenge, no matter how far or how deep you want to go. And remember, as long as you are safe, there are no limits to what you can do. Who knows, you might even do something that's never been done, something that shouldn't work, even though it does.

The Backyard Bowyer

Introduction

Welcome to my backyard on the beautiful island of Oahu, Hawaii in the lush (AKA humid and wet) rainforest off the Pali Highway. It is here (and anyplace else I can find a patch of flat ground) that I build my own bows for target archery and hunting.

I am fairly new to the art of building bows, and am nowhere near to being a master bowyer. Almost everything I know about making bows I had to learn by myself through trial and error, with a little help from others. The thought of building a bow may seem daunting, but it takes very little in the way of tools and materials to build a simple bow that will perform well.

This simplicity does have its drawbacks (which is probably why things became so complicated in the first place). If you've ever handled a compound or modern recurve bow, you know they are complicated, a complication which usually allows them to be easier to use, and can have a plethora of different parts and accessories. Simple bows have only a few different parts.

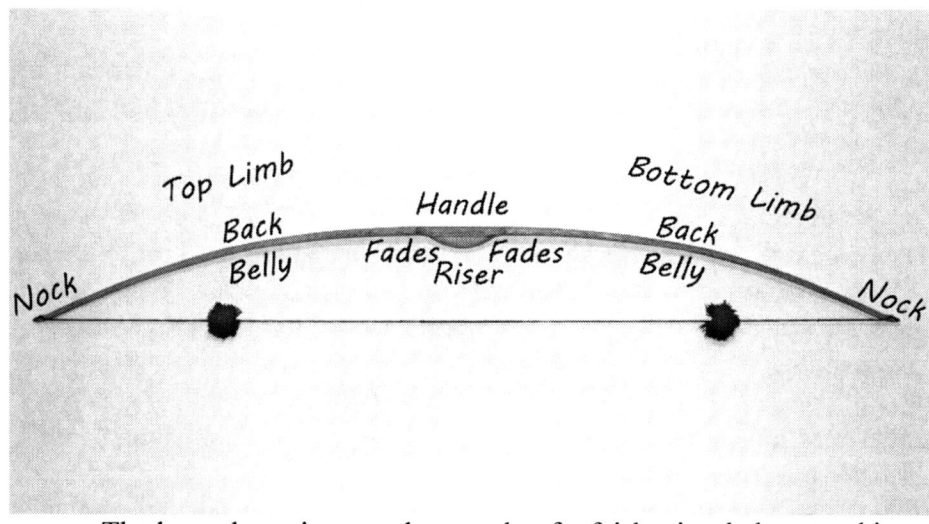

The bow above is a good example of a fairly simple bow, and in fact, it's one of the bows we'll be building in this book. On either end of the bow, left and right, are string nocks. These hold the string onto the bow, and in this case they are reinforced with tip overlays. Heading toward the center, the bulk of the bow is in the limbs. On the top edge of the picture of the bow is its back, which faces away from you when shooting the bow. The bottom of the picture, which is the part of the bow that faces you when shooting is called the belly. At the center of the bow is the handle. On either side of the handle are what are called fades or fade-outs, which rise up to the handle section itself, also called the riser.

Now that you're familiar with the bow itself, one thing that really helped me when I got started was knowing how a bow actually works. Until I figured that out, none of my first attempts at bow making were successful. A bow is, at its core, a spring. Pull back on the string, you force the limbs to flex back, storing your energy in the bow's limbs. Release the string, the stored energy in the bow's limbs is released, forcing the string forward, transferring energy into the arrow.

In order for a bow's limbs to store energy, they need to be able to bend evenly. To show you what I mean, get a ruler if you have one, if not a straight stick of even diameter will work. Place the center of the ruler on the edge of a desk, then push the tips down. This mimics drawing a bow, with you holding the center and pulling the string, which pulls back

The Backyard Bowyer

the tips. Notice how the ruler bends mainly in the center. Now, the stick or ruler doesn't want to bend, but by putting pressure in the center and the ends, it forces the ruler to bend, just as if it were an untillered bow or straight board.

The center of the ruler is under incredible stress, and pushing it too far, especially if it's of the wooden variety, will snap it very close to that center. A bow like this cannot bend very far before breaking, because the force being put on it is too great in one area, and because it can't bend very far, it can't store much energy. In order to fix this, the force of the bow bending needs to be spread out evenly, or at least in smaller sections.

By increasing the force exerted on the tips, which are normally under very little stress, the area between them and the handle will bend, and the collective bending of the whole bow will allow it to bend farther than if it were simply bending in the center. In order for the bow to bend smoothly, the bow must either get progressively thinner towards the tips, or progressively thicker towards the handle enough to counter the excess pressure put on the center.

Leaf springs work on the second idea. Spring steel bars of ever shorter lengths are bolted together so that when the spring is flexed, it flexes like a bow. This distributes the force across the whole of the spring, not just in one area. Most bows work by the first idea (which is basically the same as the second), where there is less wood at the tips than at the handle. This allows the bow to achieve its bend, and its optimal energy storage.

Another thing to consider is that the material used will determine many characteristics of your finished bow. We will be dealing with board bows, which are bows built from milled lumber, not whole logs or split logs, though the same principles apply. These boards can be purchased online from many bow-making supply shops and lumber mills specializing in the bowyer's craft for varying prices. Or with a bit of searching, quality board lumber can be found in nearly any lumber yard or home improvement store.

Among different species of wood, there are many variations that all affect what kind of bows can be built from them. For example, spruce, which is a very soft and spongy wood, usually yields very low weight bows of five to fifteen pounds at six feet in length, and usually fail with round bellies or thick limbs. Hickory, which is very resilient though not all that dense, usually yields bows that are capable of being made short with high weights and rarely fail even with rounded backs and bellies. On the far end, woods like ipe and ebony are so dense that they must be made thin and narrow, and usually must be backed with something more resilient like say, hickory, to keep them from pulling themselves apart.

And even with these, there are exceptions. It's more important to find a good quality piece of wood than to look for a certain species of wood. One of my best bows was made from a pine furring strip that cost $1.98. It was very unusual for pine, and much more dense than even most red oak. When it comes to selecting wood for the bows in this book, most hardwoods and exceptional pieces of softwoods will work well.

One of the main factors for finding boards is the relationship between late and early growth rings in the wood itself. Take a look at a piece of red oak, like this one.

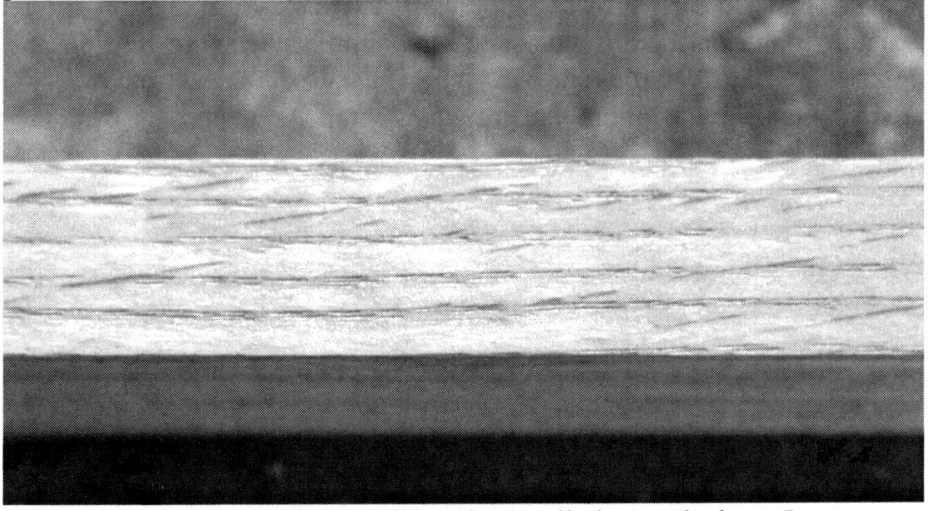

The alternating bands of wood are called growth rings. In areas with distinct seasons, these rings represent one year's growth. In wood like oak, ash, and other similar hardwoods, there is a big difference between what is called late and early growth. Early growth is the spongy looking material between the darker, denser late growth. Early growth is deposited rapidly, and the late growth is deposited slowly over the course of the year.

In certain hardwoods like maple and poplar, the difference between late and early growth is not nearly as drastic. Maple is a good example of this, as there is almost no separation between growth rings, as opposed to oak. Regardless of what type of wood, the thicker the rings are in general, and the more late growth as compared to early growth, the better.

In softwoods like spruce, pine, and yew, late and early growth rings are nearly equal in quality. In these woods, the closer together the rings are, the denser the wood, and the better they usually perform.

Here are some examples of wood, just as a visual reference when looking for boards.

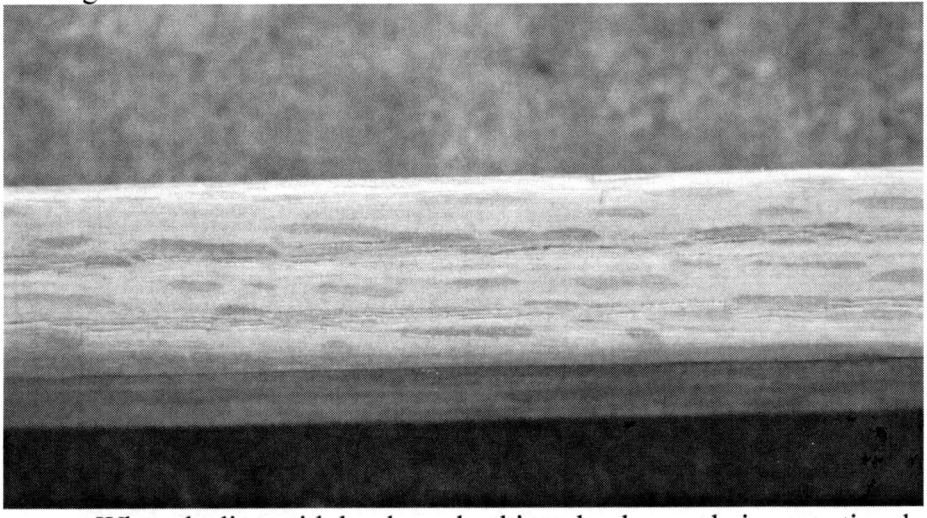

When dealing with hardwoods, this red oak sample is exceptional. At first glance it almost looks like one solid piece, though it is really three growth rings in a three quarter inch space. The early growth is nearly invisible, and the grain and growth rings run straight.

The Backyard Bowyer

With softwoods, this is what to look for. If you look closely, you will see at least fifty growth rings running through this one and a half inch wide board. This piece is out of ordinary, one of about two hundred boards at a hardware store, but they are out there. It was denser than most red oak I've run across, and performed very well as a bow.

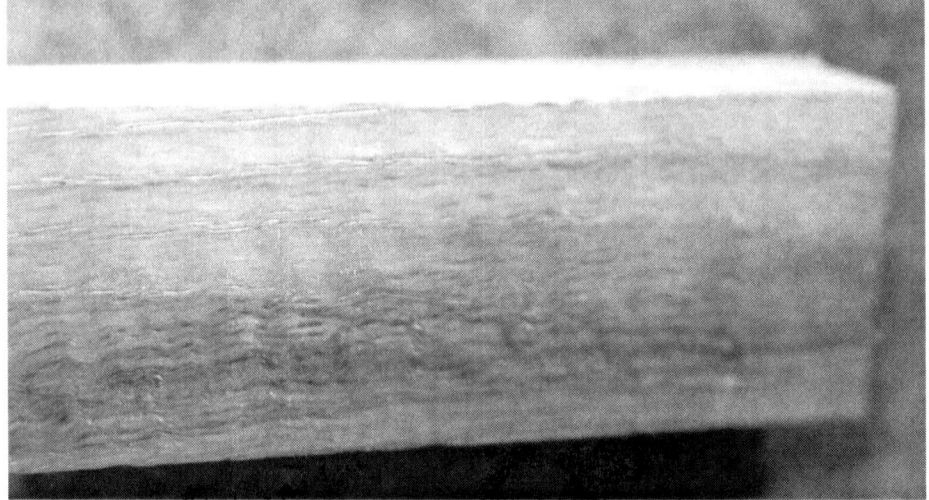

This piece here would make a very nice handle, though very bad bow limbs. Notice how the growth rings are mainly straight, but there appears to be a waviness in the wood? This wavy appearance, also called curl or figure, is usually an attractive quality in wood, something that most woodworkers look for when selecting stock. With bows, however, this wavy grain presents many weak spots, so that when the bow bends, the chances are much higher that the bow will splinter and fail. Knots should also be avoided in the working parts of the bow, though figured pieces glued onto the handle and tips more than make up for limbs with boring grain.

Now that we've got a basic understanding of bows and wood, lets get started with getting to know the tools and supplies to begin building your own bows.

Tools

There are a whole plethora of tools available for bow-making, and my suggestion is to try them all. These are the tools I use, and while most may not be traditional, they work for me. They also have the added benefit of being either very cheap or easily obtained. All you really need to start is something to cut wood with, even just a knife. An entire bow can be made from start to finish with a knife, from roughing to finishing, though some specialized tools do make thing a lot easier.

The Stanley© Surform® rasp is my favorite and most-used tool. I use it for roughing, shaping, tillering, and shaping nocks and handles. It's shaped like a plane, and I like to think of it as a plane and rasp combined. It has the control of and leaves a fine finish like a plane, but can remove lots of wood quickly like a rasp.

The Backyard Bowyer

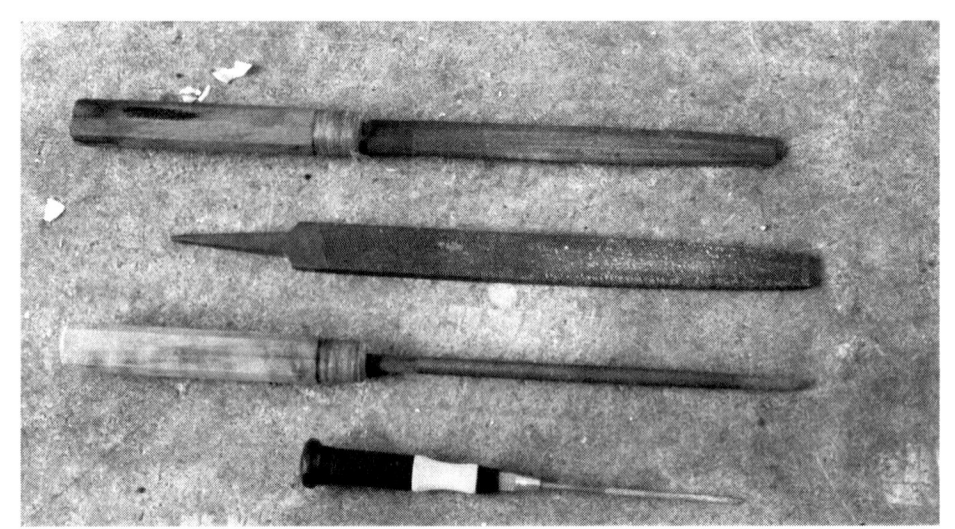

I use bastard, half-round, and rat tail files. The bastard is good for shaping nocks as well as knocking off corners and taking dried glue drips off of a bow. The half round file is used for shaping curves in the fade-outs near the handle, any inside curves, and for cleaning out integral arrow rests. The rat tail file is great for cutting nocks and string grooves.

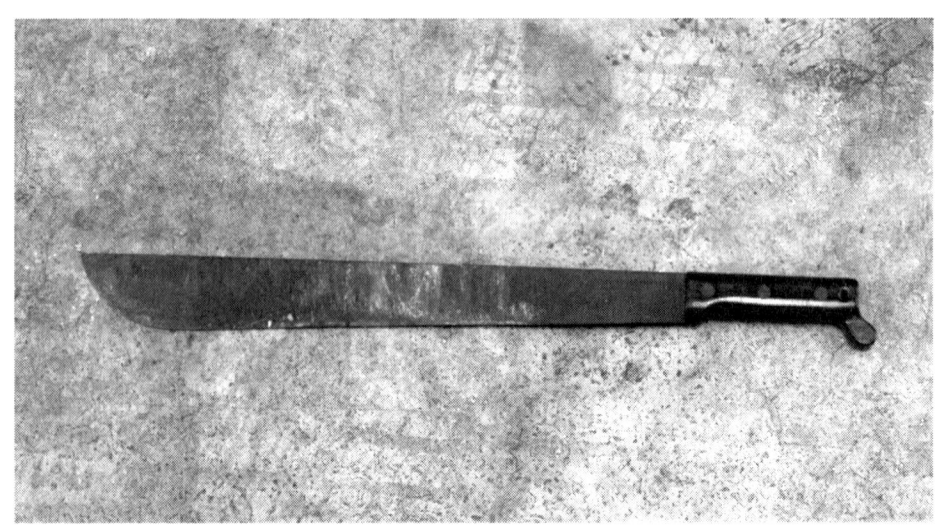

A draw knife would be very useful for removing wood quickly, but in the place of one I use an old machete. I don't suggest it, it would probably be better to buy a draw knife, especially if you can find a good one used. I only keep about four inches of the middle of the blade sharp. Any large knife will do, and make sure to keep your fingers off the edge.

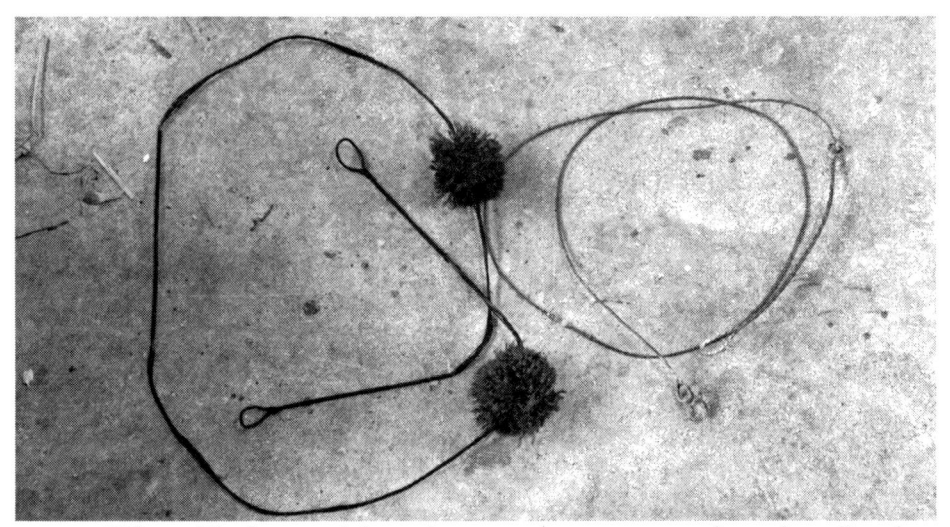

When tillering, and for using your bow, you need a string. For the very early stages of tillering, you need a string that is just a bit longer than your bow. Parachute cord or an extra-long bow string works well. If your local archery shop makes custom strings, a single-loop Flemish twist string will work well for tillering. Just tie the loose end onto the bow's nock with a timber hitch and slip the loop on.

When it comes to strings for shooting, I would suggest buying a string either online or at an archery shop. If you would rather make your own strings, check out the Bonus Track in the back of the book. Most strings nowadays are made of Dacron or Polyester, and these work well. Avoid the newer synthetics as they will definitely overpower your bow and cause it to break, or at least lower its lifespan. When buying a string, make sure that it is rated at a breaking strength at least four times the weight of your bow, though a thicker string is better than a thinner one.

A fifty pound bow would need a string of around 200 to 250 pounds, which comes out to about seven strands of Dacron, or fourteen to sixteen strands of linen. I usually just buy Dacron strings from fourteen to sixteen strands for most bows, as they are thick enough to be comfortable

The Backyard Bowyer

to use and strong enough to be used on virtually any straight bow.

Sandpaper is also a good thing to have. Sandpaper comes in many grits, and a good idea is to have a nice range of them. About 60-100, 12-180, 220-320, and 400-600 is a good range of grits to have. Look around, as many professional woodworkers throw barely used paper away, like the sanding disks in the picture.

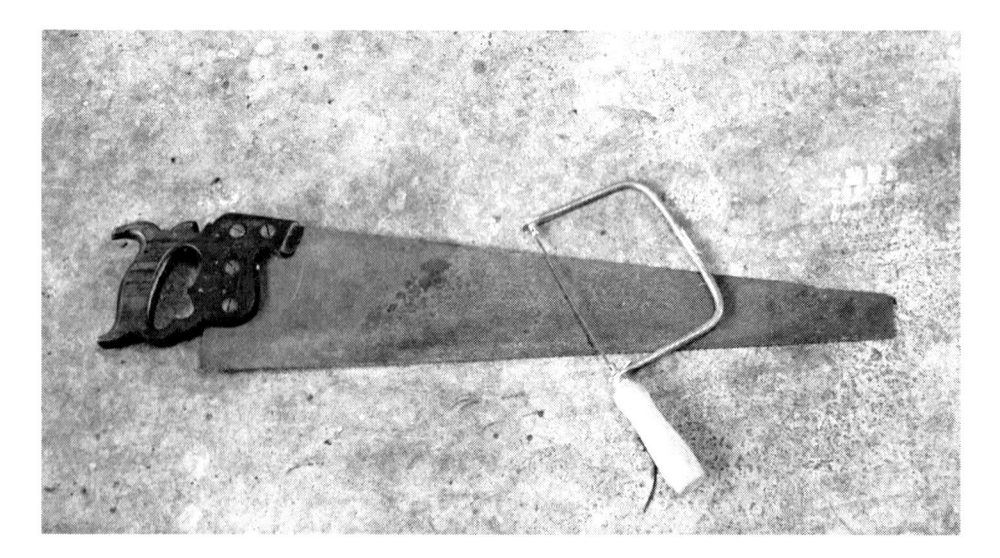

A good saw allows for the cutting of pieces of wood to length, and a coping or hacksaw makes cutting fine detail possible. I use a carpenter's saw for cutting square edges and for ripping boards. My coping saw sees use cutting nocks, dowels for arrow rests, and for cutting handle shapes as well as integral arrow rests.

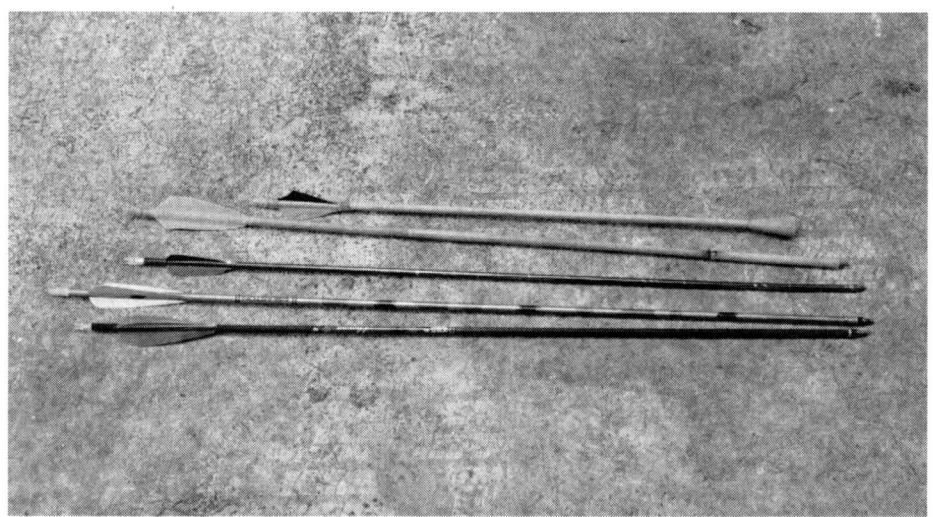

Arrows also play a big part in building bows. You should never dry fire a bow, unless you like watching them break or even explode. I like to have a set of fairly heavy arrows for new bows before they are made, because arrows should be matched to your bow. When buying arrows, make sure that they are properly weighted or spined to your bow's weight. That's not a 100% assurance, but it will get the arrows close.

Spine is a measurement of how stiff an arrow is, because when the arrow is fired, it flexes in the air before stabilizing. If the arrow is too stiff, it will not flex enough, and a weak arrow will flex too much. When buying arrows, make sure to ask what weight they are spined for. Most archery shops and sporting goods stores will have a chart based on bow weight, arrow length, and weight of points. Arrow length also plays a part, but in the beginning I cut all my arrows to 28 inches so I wouldn't overdraw my bows. If you really want to build your own, see the Bonus Track chapter in the back of the book.

The Backyard Bowyer

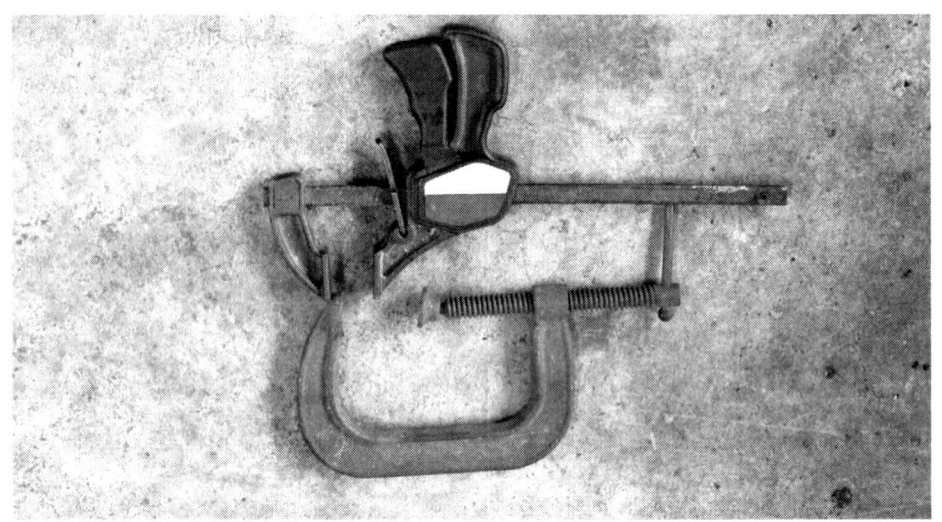

Having a couple clamps helps in those situations where you wish you had more hands. I like the ratcheting style clamps because they don't mar as much as the screw-down type, though they are more prone to slipping. A towel or piece of leather will help keep most clamps from marring your work.

Other miscellaneous supplies are a straightedge or something similar, a ruler or tape measure, glue (waterproof is a good idea), scissors, and maybe even a hammer (for the tiller, not the bows). I'll also be pulling out some tools in the book not described here. Most are easy to come by, and are explained in the chapters they appear.

Building a Tiller

I always find that I could use an extra set of hands when building bows, especially during tillering. Tillering can be done without a tiller, but it is much more difficult to see what you're doing if you are trying to do it yourself. A tiller, either just a stick or an upright tree, allows you to step back and view the bow's curve from a distance. A tillering tree also has the added advantage of doubling as a bow scale with the use of a simple bathroom scale.

This tiller, which is my current favorite type, is made of half a 2x2 and one 1x2 furring strip and finishing nails. All you need to build it is a tape measure, saw, and hammer.

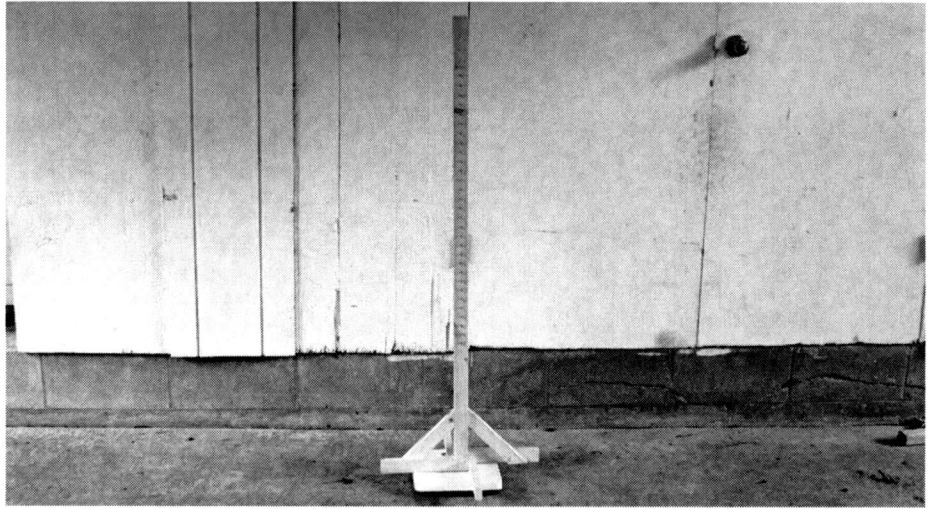

1-Tillering Stick – The basic tiller, without a stand.

2-Tillering Tree – Building a stand for the tillering stick.

3-Bow Scale – Placing a scale under the tiller to measure draw weight.

The Backyard Bowyer

Tillering Stick

To start, you need two furring strips, one 2x2 and one 1x2. Any type of wood will do as long as it is straight and is not cracking or full of knots.

Measure 48 inches on your 2x2.

Cut your furring strip down to 48 inches, making sure to make the cut as even as possible, as this will the be surface the bow sits on when in the tiller.

Measure and mark the 1x2 into six 10 inch sections, and two 5 inch sections.

Building a Tiller

The Backyard Bowyer

Cut the 1x2 into the sections you marked, making sure that the ends of the two 5 inch sections are as square as possible.

Now you can sand all of your pieces if you would like. I do this because it is very bad to get a splinter while pulling any bow on the tiller.

Here are the eight pieces sanded and ready for marking and attaching.

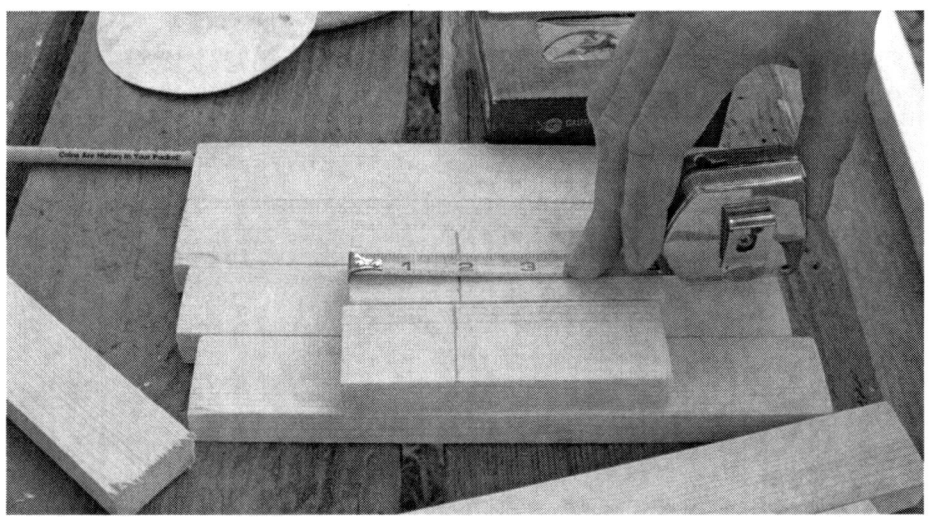

Measure 1.75 inches down from the end of each 5 inch piece, making sure each edge measures at 1.75, even if the line does not come out perfectly perpendicular to the piece.

Building a Tiller 23

The Backyard Bowyer

Line one 5 inch piece up to the side of the 2x2, with the 1.75 inch section hanging over the edge. It can be glued now, or simply nailed into place.

Hammer one nail into each corner, and then two in the center about .5 inches from the edge.

Six finishing nails are enough to secure the pieces together. If you want extra reinforcement, drill pilot holes first, as more nails may start to split the 1x2.

Line up and attach the other 5 inch piece. These two pieces hold the bow in place while it is drawn on the tiller.

Building a Tiller 25

The Backyard Bowyer

Here is the finished top of the tiller from the side, showing where the bow sits. This is the side of the tiller, and the faces connected to the 5 inch pieces are the front and rear faces.

Now you want to start marking the tiller. The reason why the two 5 inch pieces hang over the edge by 1.75 inches is because of how draw length is measured. When making and shooting bows, there are two types of draw length, the standard set by the AMO, and an older type known as true draw length. Both are measured from the point where the hand meets the handle to the point where string meets arrow when the bow is fully drawn. The only difference is that the AMO adds an extra 1.75 inches, which is what the overhang is for. Most of the time draw lengths are measured per AMO standards, which is why I use it. And besides, you are officially an Archery Manufacturer, so be proud of it!

Measure from the top of the tiller down to at least one inch over your desired draw length. If you are only going to make one bow for yourself, (good luck not getting addicted) a good way to determine your own normal draw length is to measure your height, subtract 15, then divide by 2. Add the 1.75 inches for AMO, and you have your draw length. Once you get this figure, you will need to practice and find what's comfortable for you. My calculated draw is 28.25 inches, but I usually shoot at about 27 inches.

Marking all the way down to 35 inches gives you a lot of room to experiment, as some bows can take 34 inch draws. This is really up to you, and the beauty of it is that you can always add a few inches later if you need it.

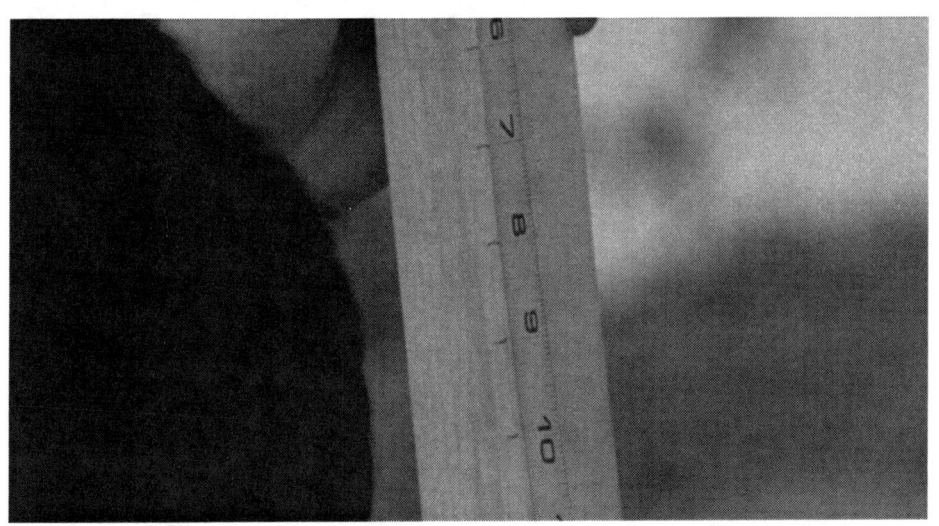

Measure and mark every inch going down, repeating on both edges of the front of the tiller.

Building a Tiller

The Backyard Bowyer

Then mark straight lines connecting both edges, so you have a sort of ladder pattern on your tiller. It is a good idea to mark the center of the tiller going down so that your nails go in a straight line.

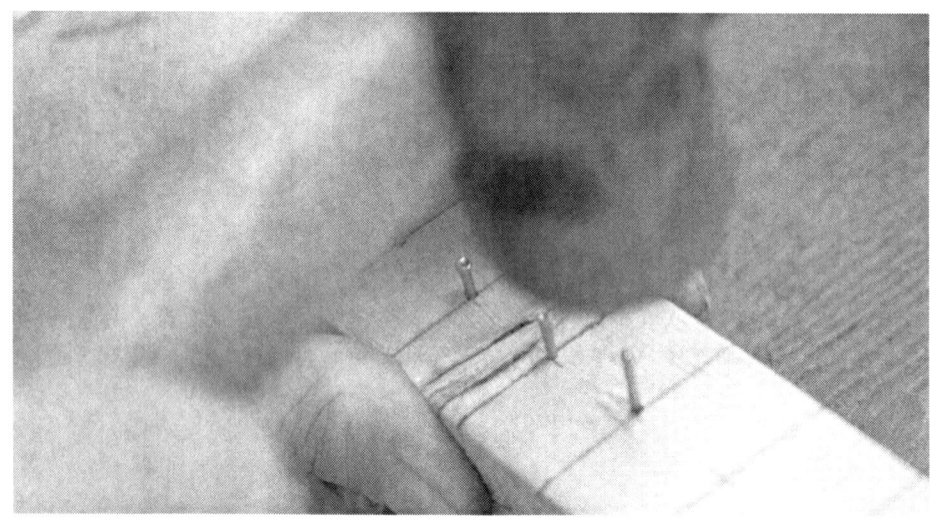

Drive finishing nails at a slight downward angle into the front of tiller following your lines until about a quarter of an inch sticks out. In place of nails, holes can be drilled and dowels glued into place.

Once all the nails are in, the main tiller is done. You could just go ahead and use it now, or you can add some legs to it. Either way, it's up to you.

Here is the finished tiller. If you're like me and want to add a stand, continue on!

Tillering Tree

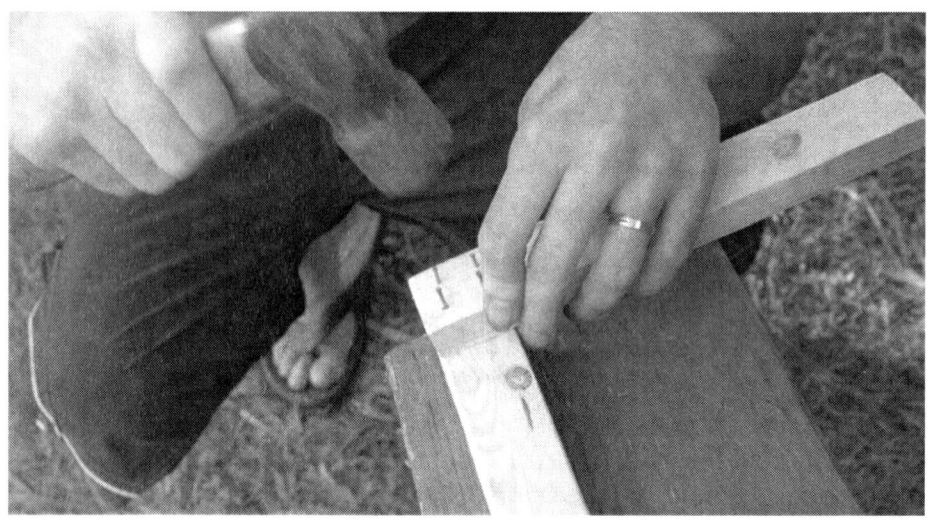

To start with the stand, hold one of the 10 inch pieces onto the edge bottom of the 2x2 like this. Nail it in place.

Turn the 2x2 over and nail another 10 inch piece on the bottom as well, until all four pieces are attached.

Once your stand is put together, you can straighten it up before putting in the final nails. Place it on a flat surface and make sure it is steady.

This is where the final nail will go. One nail goes in to each leg like this, and will help the stand hold together.

The Backyard Bowyer

Here is the finished base, and now the only thing left is to add some supports. You don't need them, but they help to keep the stand from wobbling from side to side.

Measure one and a half inches in from the end of the ten inch piece, then draw a line from the one and a half inch mark to the end.

Once you've measured and marked this diagonal line on both sides, cut the ends following the 45° line.

Line the support pieces up on the inside of the side legs so that one edge is nailed to the leg, and the other end sits flush on the tiller. Place two nails into the piece where it touches the tiller to secure it.

Building a Tiller

The Backyard Bowyer

Here is the bottom of the tiller showing the legs in relation to the tiller, and the supports to the legs. For even more stability, you could nail a solid piece of plywood or board to the bottom. Or you could ditch the stand altogether and just nail it to a wall, which will give you even more stability and a good fixed point of reference behind the tiller.

Here's the top of the tiller, where the bow goes.

The finished tiller.

Bow Scale

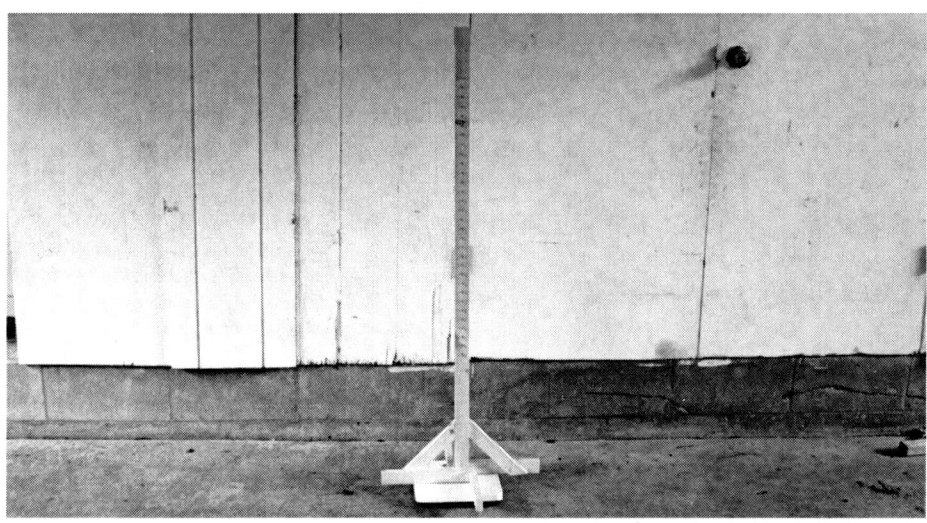

Put the tillering tree on top of a dial bathroom scale, zero it with the scale on it, and you have a decent bow scale. In order to keep readings accurate, re-calibrate the scale with the bow on it, as its weight will alter the reading.

Building a Tiller

The Backyard Bowyer

Flat Bow

    My very first bow was a flat bow with a very large, non-bending handle. My second bow was also a flat bow, but I had experimented with a very short, non-bending handle, which has become my favorite type of bow. The flat bow itself is a very simple design, in which its limbs are rectangular in cross section.

    The flat bow is a very old design, perhaps one of the oldest variations of the bent stick. Yet, the flat bow we are all familiar with, the one that lends its shape to modern longbows, recurves, and compounds, is a fairly recent design that came to popularity in the twenties. This design, which allows the flat limbs to deal with tension and compression much better than the narrow belly of the English longbow, was favored for its greater speed and ability to launch an arrow farther.

    The bow we'll be building is a simple flat bow with a non-bending handle, and at six feet long it can be made of practically any wood. There are seven different steps to building this bow.

1-Design – Finding a bow design that suits you.

2-Selecting Wood – Selecting a board for the bow.

3-Roughing the Bow – Laying out the design and bringing to shape.

4-Backing the Bow – Gluing a backing to support a questionable stave.

5-Rough Tillering – Getting the stave to bend.

6-Tillering – Bringing the bow up to its full draw and weight.

7-Finishing – Sanding, adding extras, and sealing out moisture.

Design

As I've said before, the flat bow is an old design, a design that has seen many different forms across time, cultures, and geographic locations. Because it is derived from many different places, the bows that can be grouped together as flat bows are extremely varied. What all flat bows have in common are limbs that are fairly rectangular in cross section, without the extreme rounded cross section characteristic of the English longbow and other 'stacked' bows.

By stack, I mean that the working wood in the bow is much smaller than the non-working wood. In any bow, the back undergoes incredible tension as the bow bends, the force trying to pull the back apart. On the belly of the bow, the wood is under compression, the force of tension on the back literally crushing the belly wood. This is the main reason why a bow will take set, because the back stretches a bit and the belly crushes a bit.

Only a small amount of wood is actually under this stress of tension and compression. The bulk of the wood in a bow is dead, it doesn't do any work, just adds weight and body. The relatively wide, thin limbs of a flat bow maximize the amount of working wood, as opposed to the thin strip of working wood in rounded or half-rounded bows. These bows can be safely made shorter than similar bows of a rounded cross section.

Flat bows come in an extremely wide range of limb styles. These are five main variations on limb shape that I use regularly.

The first is what is called a pyramid bow. It is very wide near the handle, around two inches or more and then tapers rapidly to the end, like a pyramid. This shape takes care of most of the tillering needed, and as a result, the bow's thickness is fairly uniform its whole length.

The second is what I call the half pyramid, and is similar to how I make English style longbows. It tapers down much like the pyramid, yet

The Backyard Bowyer

not as much, and requires shaping the belly as well to obtain a correct tiller.

The third is a full flat bow. Its limbs are almost full-width the whole way toward the tips. At about three fourths down the limb, it tapers down to the tip's width. This style of bow requires a great deal of belly removal near the center of each limb to attain the correct tiller. This style tends to get more weight and speed out of most woods, but it is tricky.

The fourth style is rather interesting, and based off of a couple of known prehistoric European bows. It is similar to the last flat bow, except the last one fourth of the limb cuts down sharply to a narrow width. On the belly, wood is removed in the center of the limb, but the tip is left thick to compensate for it being very narrow. It is a very eye-catching style of bow.

The fifth style, and my personal favorite for very short bows is the paddle bow. It looks sort of like a paddle, being very wide at the middle of the limb, and rounding down to a narrow width at the tips and handle. Again, it is kind of striking and unusual, and it requires lots of belly tillering. It is quite tricky to get it right.

To further complicate things, but still on a very basic note, our bow can either have a handle section that doesn't bend, or one that does. A bending handle makes the bow do more work evenly throughout its length, which allows it to be shorter than if it has a stiff handle. With a board bow like this, a bending handle would mean that the handle section cannot be glued on, unless it is flexible like leather or plastic, as a glued wood riser would just pop off. The energy in the handle also contributes to hand shock, which can be uncomfortable. A couple main benefits to the bending handle bow is that more weight can be obtained safely, and the bow is usually a little faster than the draw weight would indicate.

A stiff handle on a bow reduces most hand shock, because there is little energy stored in the handle. In a board bow, a stiff handle allows you to glue on an extra piece of wood to make the riser more comfortable, though the fades around the riser need to be cut down into the bow wood, reducing its thickness and ultimately its final draw weight. Another option is to glue on a handle upon the full-thickness board and wrap it in place, though I notice this usually produces very disconcerting ticking sounds when shooting the bow. One of the benefits to a non bending handle is ease of use compared to a bending handle bow. There is also a possibility of cutting an arrow shelf into the bow itself as opposed to gluing on an arrow rest or having none at all.

Another consideration is length. For a first bow, I suggest starting with a six foot board, and cutting the nocks at 70 inches. This length is extremely forgiving, and in most bows, even somewhat major flaws can go overlooked and pose no real threat to the bow's lifespan. The downside to this length is that the bow's draw weight will be much lower than if it were, say, 66 inches, because there is more wood working, and the limbs are under less stress.

A shorter bow will be under greater stress and will need to be made thinner than a longer bow at the same draw weight. This increase in stress also increases the chances of the bow breaking, and shorter lengths are much, much less forgiving of tillering flaws. Building shorter bows is a good test of your skill, as shorter bows do have an increased practical value for hunting and target archery. A bending-handle bow can also be made a little shorter than a stiff handled bow with the same performance, usually by the same amount as the non bending handle (if your non-bending handle is four inches long, taking four inches off of the bow is still in a safe range).

Yet another consideration is the shape of the string nocks, which is where the string attaches to the bow. There are three basic nock shapes I use: traditional nocks (which are traditional for most modern longbows), pin nocks, and v-nocks.

The Backyard Bowyer

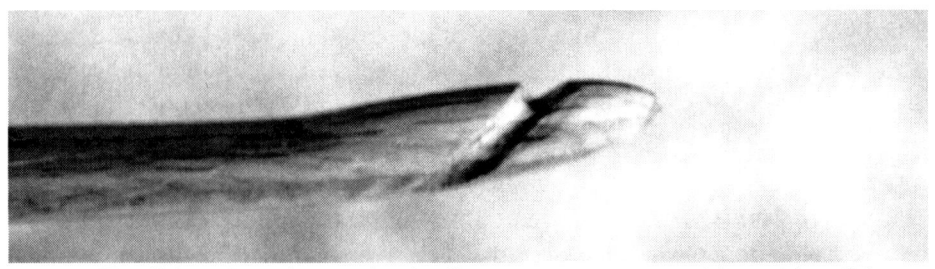

Traditional nocks are basically two grooves on either side of the nock at a 45 degree angle which may or may not connect around the nock. These hold the string well, though shallow grooves may cause the string to slip easily, especially if the bow is inadvertently knocked or dropped. These nocks also include the deeper nocks of English longbows as well as the wider nocks of most modern flat bows.

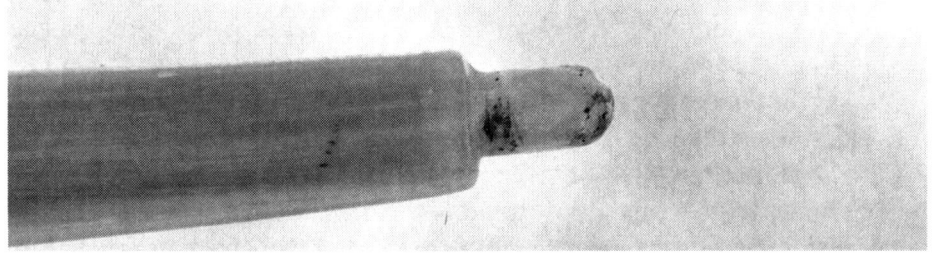

Pin nocks are very simple, consisting of a raised pin surrounded on one or more sides by a shelf of wood that the string rests on. This can be achieved by cutting the shelf, or even gluing and wrapping wood, bone, plastic, leather, etc. to the end of an untouched nock. The first type of pin nock usually can weaken the tip of the bow, and the second is probably the most sturdy, as material is being added, not taken away. The second type is also great for shortening a bow's nock to nock length without any permanent cutting, which is useful for testing how far a bow can be shortened.

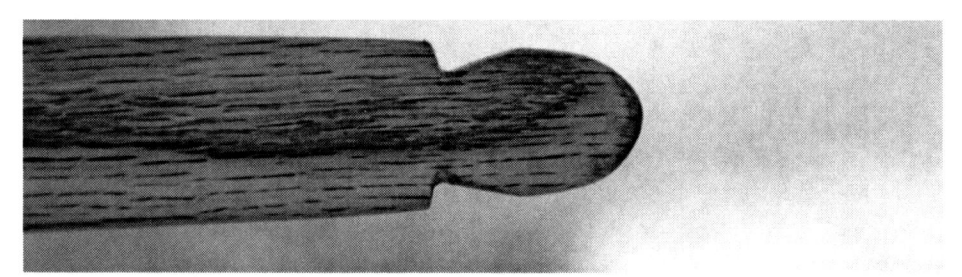

V-nocks (or at least that's what I call them) are simple to make and have the added benefit of preventing the string from slipping off of the nock in either direction. In a v-nock, the string is basically held in a v cut on one or both sides of the nock, which serves to keep the string in place regardless of any bumps or even harsh overdraws. This type of nock goes well with paddle-bows.

Due to its ease of tillering and because it uses narrower board stock of 1x2 (three quarters by one and a half inches), the bow we'll be doing is of the half pyramid style. It will have a non-bending handle with a glued on riser and traditional nocks. It will also start out with 72 inch (six foot) board stock and have a finished nock to nock length of 70 inches. This is a very simple bow, and is a great candidate for your first. Once you've given it a try, most any other design mentioned here will be a breeze.

The Backyard Bowyer

Selecting Wood

Red oak is one of my favorite types of wood for bows, mainly because it's cheap and I can find it here in Hawaii. Most board lumber will make good bows, provided the grain is straight. As long as the bow is made well, and heavy draw weights aren't important, even $1.00 spruce furring strips make very good, albeit very weak bows.

This board is not perfect, but it will make a good bow with a backing. A backing will keep the surface of the wood from splintering, which is a big problem with questionable boards. Even if a board starts to splinter slightly, a backing may save it.

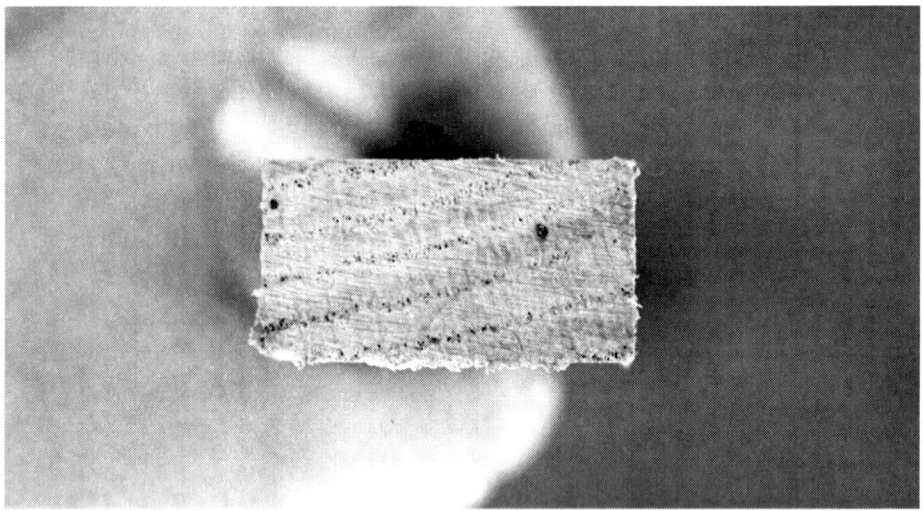

Here's the end of the board, which is an example of what's called rift-sawn lumber. The other types are quarter-sawn, in which the growth rings run vertical, and flat-sawn in which the growth rings run horizontal. All three work well, but I prefer rift and quarter because it is harder to find perfectly straight flat-sawn boards that don't have large ares where rings are broken on the surface.

Here you can also see the growth rings in this piece of wood. There are six rings in this .75 inch area, which is a good number for red oak. I like six or less rings per .75 inches on hardwoods, and more than twenty per .75 inches in softwoods as this means denser wood.

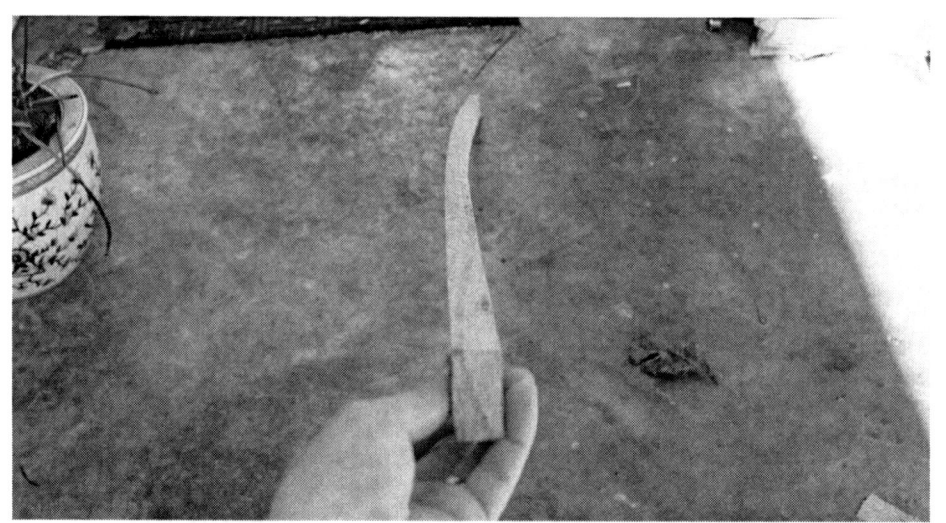

From the side you can see that the growth rings run fairly straight down the board, and run off near this tip. This is about as much run-off as should be allowed on less dense woods than oak. As long as the growth rings are dense with only a little spongy wood in-between, the grain can run off in about four or five places.

The wood's growth rings and grain should run straight, but they are very uneven and wavy in this board. It will make a good flat bow with a backing. The shorter the bow, the better your wood needs to be as it will

Flat Bow 43

The Backyard Bowyer

be under more stress.

One thing this board has to its advantage is that sometime after it was milled, it dried into this flexed shape. When a bow is made from a single piece of wood, the belly of the bow will get compressed permanently, and the back will be permanently stretched. This means that if your board started off perfectly straight, it will take a bend towards the belly once made into a bow.

This permanent bend is called set, and when it causes the the bow to bend past the handle towards the belly, it is called string follow. It is possible for a bow to have no or even negative string follow. Having the stave flexed towards the back of the bow like this can reduce string follow, and possibly even remove it.

This board stave is flexed less than half an inch, and I usually end up with about an inch of set. The flex in this stave should bring string follow down to about half an inch, which is pretty good. Another thing to remember is that the more the stave is flexed toward the back of the bow, the more tension and strain the wood is under, and the higher chances are that the bow will break.

Roughing the Bow

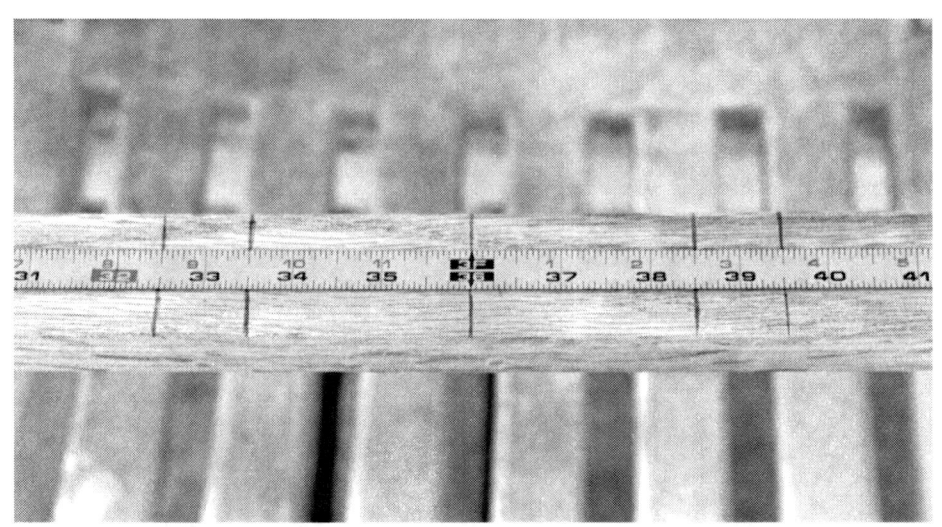

Start with a six foot board as your bow stave. Measure the center, at 36, then mark 2.5 inches from the center on both sides, and then an inch more on either side. This will become your handle.

Measure across the stave, marking the true center of the stave. From here you'll be able to line up your ends because most boards are not

Flat Bow 45

The Backyard Bowyer

perfectly straight. Simply following the board could result in a crooked bow, which may twist and explode at full draw (I know that from personal experience).

Tie two weights onto the ends of a length of string slightly longer than your bow. Drape this string from end to end, making sure the line is taut.

Adjust the string on the ends until the string lines up straight through the center of the handle.

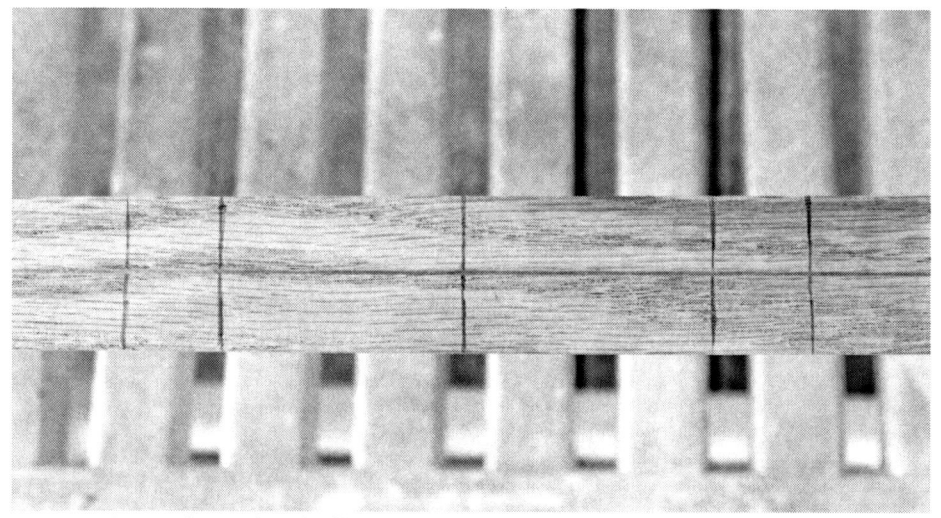

Once the string is lined up through the center, mark where is is along all marked points and the ends. This is your true center, so that when you cut your bow from the stave, the tips will line up.

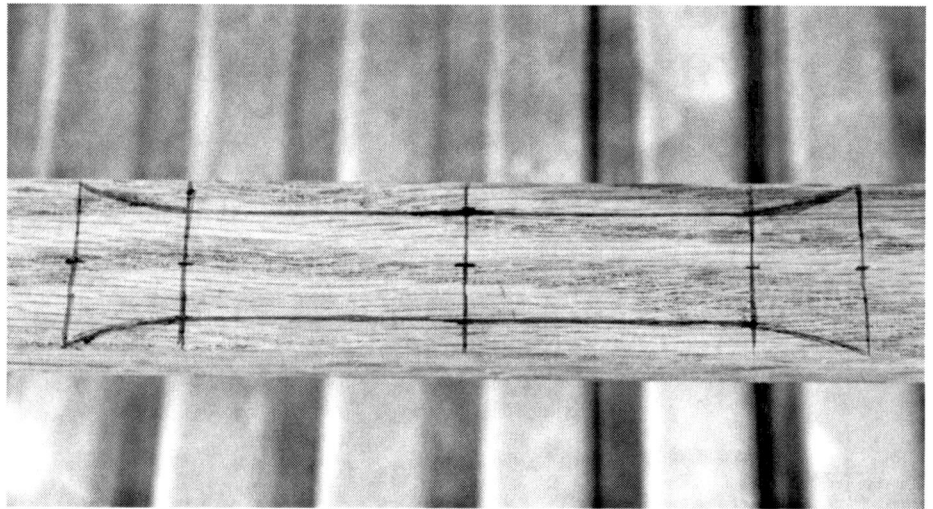

Mark an inch centered over each center point, or half an inch on

Flat Bow 47

The Backyard Bowyer

either side of the center points. Connect the lines in the center, then draw a smooth curve from the thinner section to the full width. This will become the bow's handle.

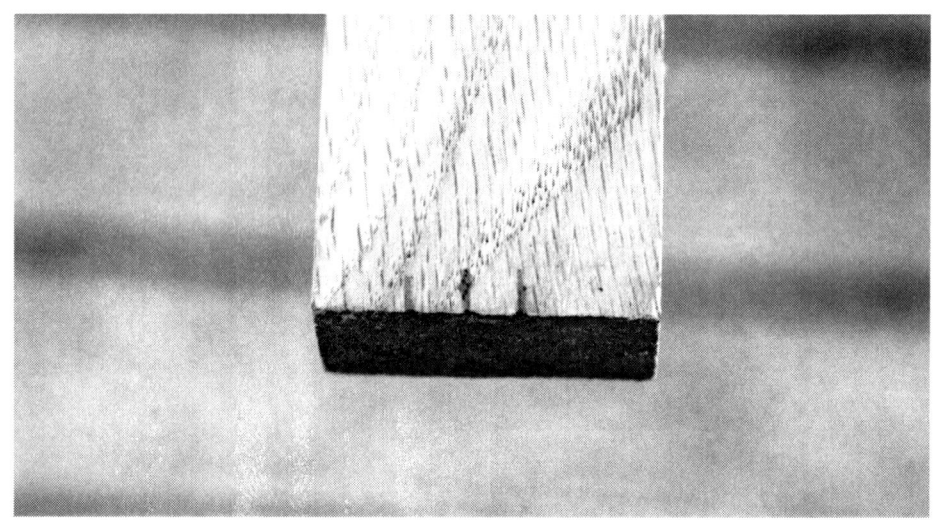

Mark the ends of the stave at half an inch, centered over the center mark.

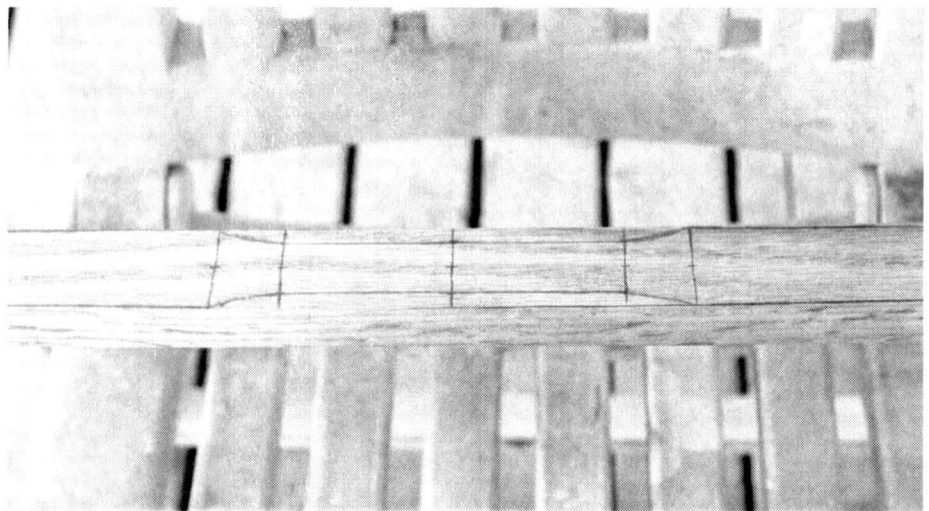

With a straightedge, draw lines connecting the ends of the handle to the tips of the stave.

This is the basic shape of the bow, which is our half-pyramid shape. This is the easiest type of limb shape to work with, though it is a fairly light weight design. Weight and speed can be added by keeping the limbs full width up to 75% of the limb's length, like the full flat bow.

Here is a closeup of one limb.

Flat Bow   49

The Backyard Bowyer

And the other.

Once the shape of the bow is laid out, it's ready to be shaped down. A workbench or table works well to support the stave, but if you don't have either to use, a chair with arms works well too. The chair also gives the added advantage of giving an open space in the middle of your work, allowing more freedom of movement when using a rasp or Surform®.

If you have one, a railing works well as it also gives freedom of movement. Use two clamps, or have somebody support the end of the stave you aren't working on if you only have one, as the stave may move around with only one clamp.

With the Surform®, shave one edge of the stave down to the line. Doing it this way is much easier than trying to shave it straight down. Make sure to take even strokes in only one direction with the Surform®.

Flat Bow

The Backyard Bowyer

Once down to the line, start bringing the other side down. Once both sides are even, shave the wood lightly with the Surform® held straight onto the stave just enough to even it out. Don't remove too much wood now, as any further touch ups can be done later.

Now that this half of one limb is done, it's time to do it all over again. It helps to put a wedge under the stave when shaping the other side as the unclamped side tends to stick up into the air, making shaping very,

very difficult.

With the stave roughed down, the stave is looking more like a bow.

Clamp the stave up and shape down the handle. I use a combination of a half round file and Surform®, but there is a half-round blade for the Surform® that works just as well.

Flat Bow 53

The Backyard Bowyer

Start by filing or rasping two half-round grooves into the handle, bringing them down to your guide lines. It helps to cut these like the limbs, starting on one edge, bringing it down to the line. Then flatten it out and clean it up.

With the Surform®, rasp straight across, perpendicular to the stave, and shape the handle down. This goes pretty quick, especially if you cut one edge down and then finish it.

Starting a little past where the handle starts to get thinner, mark 5/8 of an inch on the side of the handle. The back of the stave is on the bottom in the picture.

These marks will become your fade outs, or fades. That's where the handle thins out into the limbs.

Flat Bow   55

The Backyard Bowyer

Just like with the handle, start by filing or rasping the radius near the handle. Try to keep the radius fairly flat, as this will keep the bend a little farther from the handle once the stave starts bending.

Rough the belly of the bow down to 5/8 of an inch. The best way to get this measurement even is to measure 5/8 every inch or so and connect the marks.

Here is the stave with the limbs roughed to 5/8 of an inch thick.

A closeup of the handle. That pronounced curve from the fades will keep the handle from bending, allowing a riser to be glued onto the handle.

Flat Bow 57

The Backyard Bowyer

Here is the rough stave, ready for backing. Looks a lot like my nifty half-pyramid sketch, doesn't it?

Backing the Bow

Lightly sand the back of the bow, just enough to slightly rough the surface to help glue adhere better. 120 grit works well. Once it is sanded, wipe the back of the bow down with either alcohol or water to remove any fine dust that might keep the backing from adhering.

My favorite backing for board staves is fiberglass drywall tape. It

Flat Bow

The Backyard Bowyer

is self-adhesive, which makes applying it to the back of a bow much easier than non-adhesive backings, and it is very tough. It is not strong enough to overpower the belly of a bow, but just enough to keep splinters down on less-than-perfect staves. If you cannot find drywall tape, or don't like the appearance of it, there are other options for backing materials.

Virtually any cloth makes a good backing. My most used are linen, burlap, silk, and hemp. Of these, silk and burlap are my favorites. Silk can be found in old clothing, as well as most fabric stores. It has the benefit of not only holding down splinters, but also reducing the effects of string follow. Burlap is also high on my list because it can be had for free in the form of bags, or cheap at most fabric stores and even Wallyworld. It works much like hemp or linen on a bow, but has a much more primitive feel to it, and makes a great natural camouflage.

You can also use cotton, denim, canvas, polyester, or any other cloth for backing, though these usually won't help a bow that is already developing splinters. Even paper makes a decent backing just to help keep splinters from forming.

Once you've decided on a backing, place it on the back of the bow. With drywall tape, stick it on one tip, then press it down and slide your fingers across the stave so that the tape goes on tight without any slack spots. With any other backing, I like to tape the ends down onto the belly of the bow, over the tips. Just make sure the backing is fairly tight over the back of the bow.

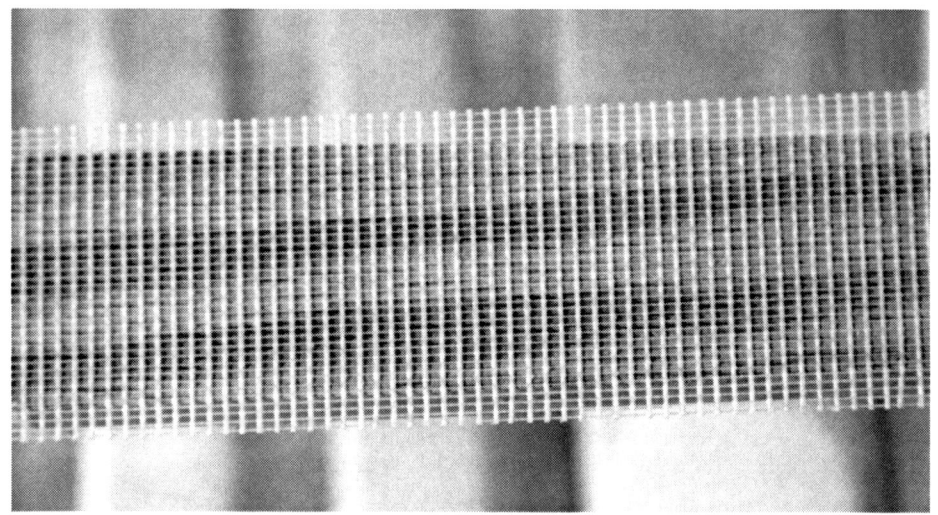

A closeup of the tape before gluing.

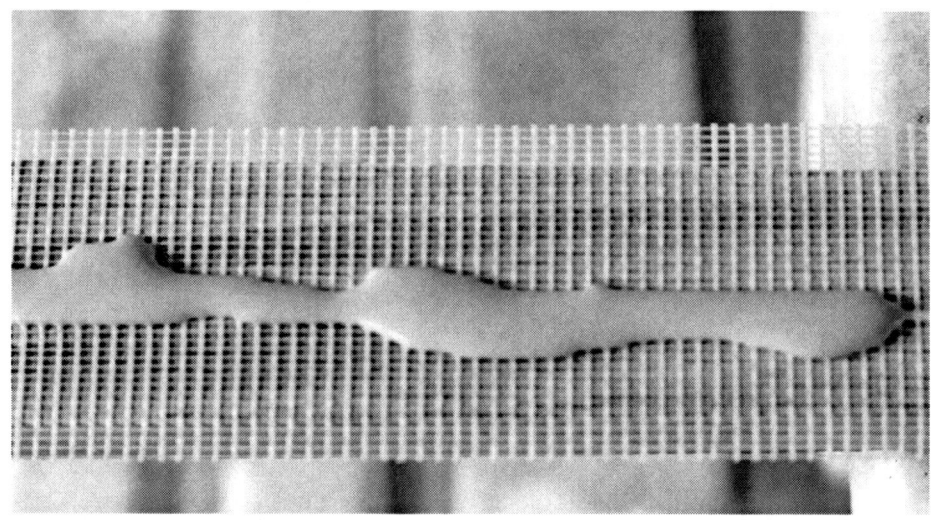

Lay a line of glue down the back of the bow, on top of the backing. For paper and thick fabric, you want to spread some glue onto the back of the bow first, before taping the backing down.

Flat Bow 61

The Backyard Bowyer

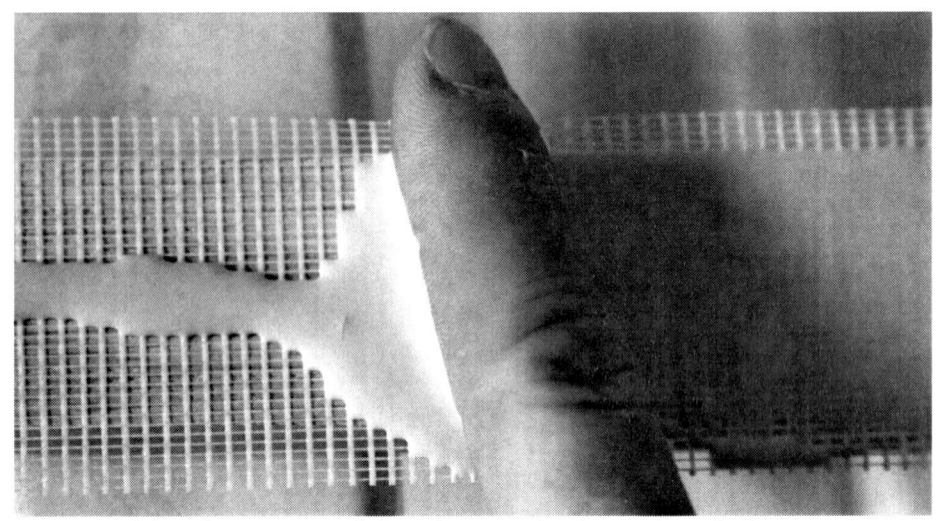

With a finger, spread the glue evenly down the whole stave in one direction. Make sure the glue is on evenly without any thick, runny spots.

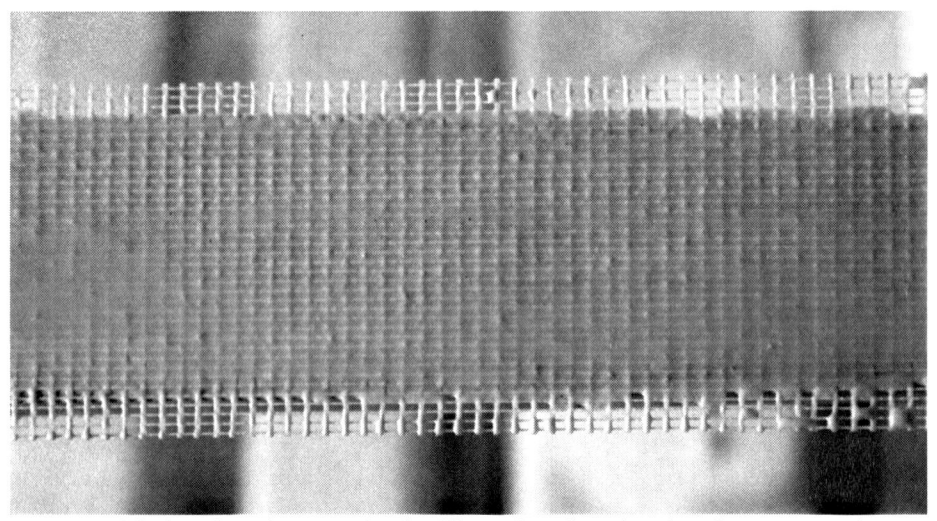

This is what the tape looks like after the glue has been spread. Let the stave dry overnight.

A closeup of the dry backing. I like how the wood is still visible under the drywall tape, which is one reason I use it.

Once the stave is dry, cut the excess backing with a sharp knife or the Surform®. If using drywall tape, be very careful, and wear gloves as glass fibers can make you very itchy. Also be sure to wear good lung protection and don't rub your eyes (again, I speak from experience). Now the stave is ready for tillering.

Flat Bow

The Backyard Bowyer

Rough Tillering

The first step to tillering is the see if the stave bends. Hold the stave like this, with the back of the stave pointing towards the ground, and push down on the handle like this. You can see the limb is flexing a little. See that a lot of the flex is near the handle, not in the middle of the limb or tips. This is not what we're looking for.

64

Lightly take wood off from the middle of the limb and the tip, keeping the area near the handle untouched. Work lightly and keep checking the stave for bend, as you can't add wood back once its been taken off.

Once the limb bends more evenly toward the middle like this, we can move on to tillering with a long string.

Flat Bow

The Backyard Bowyer

Mark half an inch from the end of the tip of both limbs on the back and sides.

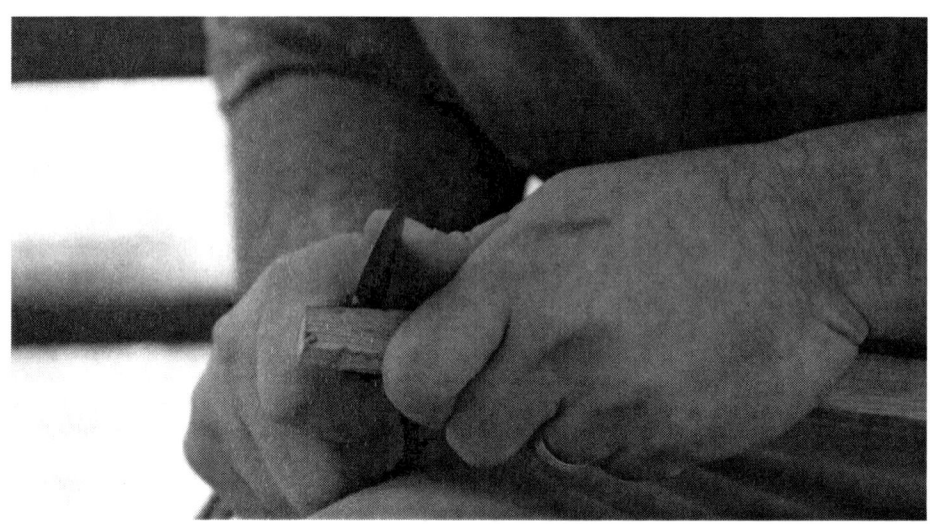

Using a rat tail file or knife, cut notches on the sides and back of the tip. If using a knife, it helps to use pushing v-cuts and peeling cuts, kind of like peeling an apple.

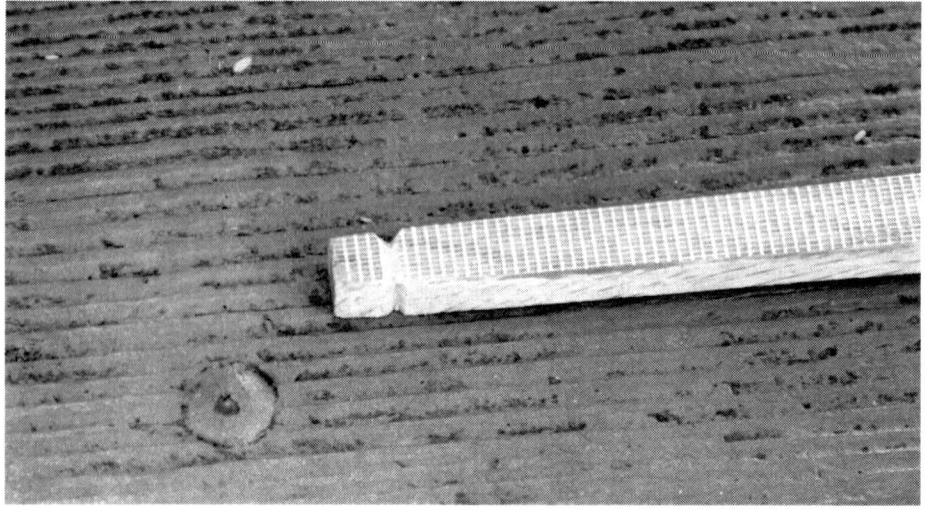

This groove should run across the sides and back of the bow.

Using your long tillering string, which is a length of parachute cord in this picture, place it on the bow loose. Place the bow in the tiller, and then pull the string until the limbs flex about an inch. Return the bow back to rest, then back up to one inch. This is called exercising the bow, and it helps the wood get used to bending.

Pull until the bow bends about two inches, then set it back to rest. Be sure to exercise the bow every time the bow is drawn further than it

The Backyard Bowyer

has been before, and every time wood is removed. Constantly exercising the limbs, about thirty to fifty times each time, will help keep set low and prevent the bow breaking. This also helps prevent splinters on the back, and chrysals on the belly.

Set the string until there is no slack, but don't brace the bow yet.

Pull the string back to about 13 inches, exercising every two to three inches or so. Then begin drawing the bow further, an inch at a time, exercising every inch.

At 22 inches on this bow are the first signs of a tillering problem. Problems will arise at different times, but dealing with them is the same regardless of how they show up. Problems usually don't show up with the long string as the bow is under very little stress.

Flat Bow 69

The Backyard Bowyer

See how much the right limb is bending, especially near the handle? This limb is too weak near the handle, and weak in general. To fix this, the area near the tip needs to be thinned.

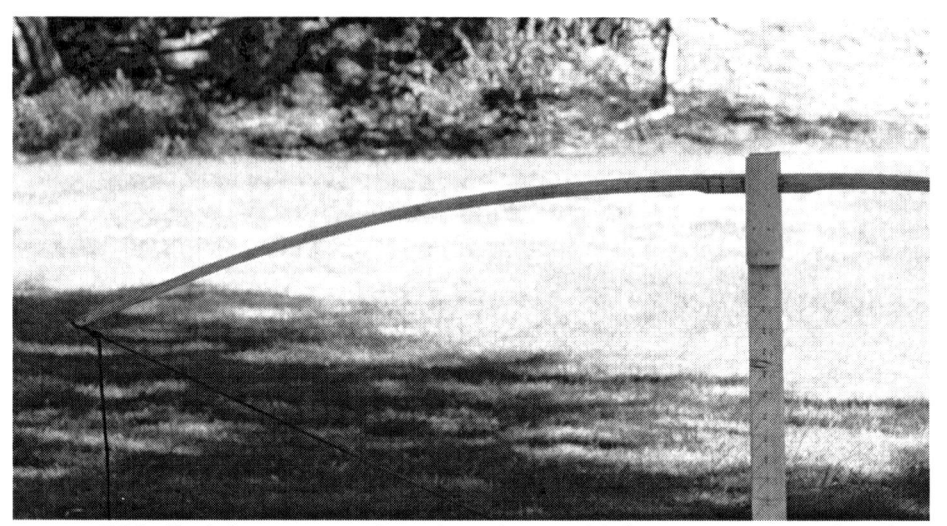

This limb is stronger than the other and it has a more even bend, as opposed to the other limb bending close to the handle. To fix this, remove a little wood evenly on this entire limb.

Once the limbs have been evened out, continue drawing the string further. At 24 inches, the limbs should bend mostly near the center of both limbs, away from the handle. The bow should be tillered up to its full draw, which for me is 28 inches. From 24 to 28 inches is a big step, and where a bow is most likely to break.

Here's the bow at 25 inches.

Flat Bow

The Backyard Bowyer

Here's 26 inches, and the left limb needs to be shaved down slightly. Try to keep both limbs even.

At 27 inches, the left limb is still too stiff.

With the left limb slightly weakened, the curve is much more even. At this point, it is alright for one limb to be just a little more stiff than the other.

At 28 inches, this is about where you want the bow's curve to be. Once the bow is braced, the curve will appear to be sharper, especially near the tips. This is because right now the string is pulling down on the bow's tips, but once braced, the string will pull inward as well.

Full draw with the long string pulls on the bow less than with a normal length string. Because of this, check the draw weight of the bow now with the scale, as this should be your minimum finished weight.

Flat Bow 73

The Backyard Bowyer

Tillering

Mark an inch in from the end of the bow on the back edge, then draw a 45 degree line down towards the handle. This is where the string nock will be.

Just like with the long string groove, cut or file the string nock, except this time don't cut into the top.

The long string grooves made earlier make a great bow stringer for stringing the bow up safely. To use it, place the top loop of the short string over one nock, then slide it down the bow so that the bottom loop can go onto the nock. Place the ends of the long string into the string grooves, then step on the middle of it. Pull the bow up, and as the limbs get pulled down, you can easily slip the top loop of the string over the nock.

Flat Bow

The Backyard Bowyer

Here's the bow at full brace, which is about six inches of space from the back of the handle riser to the string.

From here we will tiller to 24 inches, then work the bow in a little before bringing it to full draw.

Pull the string down to 10 inches, exercising it from brace to ten about thirty times, then pull it up to 11 and repeat. Exercise the limbs every time the bow reaches a new length of draw.

12 inches.

13 inches.

Flat Bow 77

The Backyard Bowyer

15 inches.

17 inches.

18 inches.

19 inches.

Flat Bow 79

The Backyard Bowyer

20 inches. On this bow, a weak spot, known as a hinge, has developed on the right limb. To fix it, the left limb and the area around the hinge need to be shaved down.

21 inches.

80

22 inches. Another hinge is starting to form on the left limb. Every inch of draw can bring out hidden flaws.

22 inches.

Flat Bow 81

The Backyard Bowyer

23 inches.

24 inches. Now it's time to work the bow in a little. When shooting the bow for the first time, make sure to keep people away from you just in case the bow fails. Wear glasses or goggles to protect your eyes, and do not draw past 24 inches. Hold the handle in the middle, so that the arrow rests about an inch and a half above center on your first knuckle. The stiffer limb will be the top limb.

In order to make sure the bow isn't overdrawn, take your arrows and place a piece of tape at 24 inches, measured from the bottom of the arrow nock. Another option would be to use 24 inch arrows.

Put enough tape on the arrow so that you can feel it against your hand, as this will tell you when you've hit 24 inches. You can also put the mark at 22.25 inches so that you can draw the mark till the back of the handle. Either way works.

Flat Bow 83

The Backyard Bowyer

I suggest using a shooting glove and arm guard, as the string cuts into the fingers when drawing and causes the fingers to swell from the rolling action of the release. The string also has a tendency to slap the arm which can cause bruising, blisters, and some skin loss. I use neither, so I have large, calloused fingertips and a permanent bruise on my left arm. You have been warned.

Look at the intense expression on my face. Normally, I smile while doing this, it looks more official this way. Fire the bow at least fifty times to work it in. That may sound like a lot, but if you have 12 arrows, that's only a little more than four rounds.

Here's the bow at 26 inches. After firing the bow, these next four inches are really just to fine tune the bow and get it to full draw. Once you reach your full draw, tiller the bow an inch further just as insurance.

Flat Bow 85

The Backyard Bowyer

27 inches.

28 inches. This is my full draw, so I draw an inch further. If your draw is longer, just be sure to tiller up to that point and then an inch or so beyond it.

29 inches. Notice how the bow bends mainly near the middle of the limbs. That is where you want it to bend.

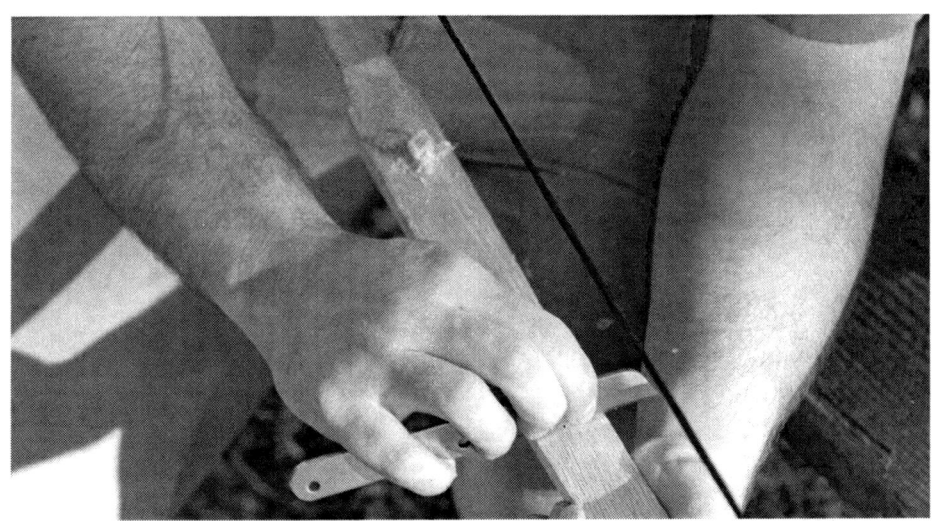

With a small knife or cabinet scraper, scrape the belly clean of tool marks, making sure to remove very little wood. Any uneven tiller can be fixed with the scraper.

The finished tiller. Especially at this longer length, stiff tips and a stiff handle will increase the power and speed of the bow. If the bow shocks the hand when shooting, the tips can be scraped a little more to soften the shock.

The Backyard Bowyer

Enjoy your new bow, and shoot it out at full draw. Make sure to fire the bow at full draw a few hundred times before letting someone else try it (personal experience again). This lets the bow settle down to its final draw weight and set. A bow is also less likely to fail in the long run if it is broken in first.

Finishing

Now that your bow is tillered, we can add a handle and tip overlays. Adding a handle riser makes the bow more comfortable to grip and shoot, especially for extended periods.

Cut a piece of wood as long as your handle.

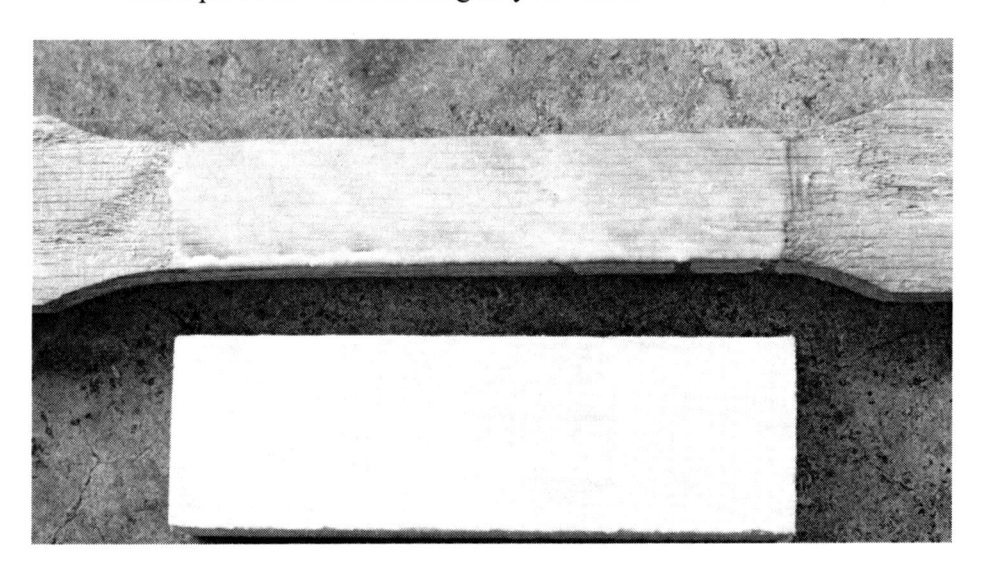

The Backyard Bowyer

After sanding both handle and riser, glue them together. You should select wood that looks good, as opposed to the boring wood in the limbs. In a non-bending handle like this, the wood should be under no real stress, so this is a good place to put some knotty, curly, quilted, burly, and other crazy grained wood not suited for bow limbs.

Clamp the handle overnight to allow it time to dry.

Once the handle is dry, take the clamps off, then clamp it to your work area (bench, railing, chair, etc.).

Shave the glued on riser down to the level of the handle.

Shave both sides down until they are even. From here we can cut the riser's shape.

The Backyard Bowyer

There are lots of possibilities for handle shapes, and this is just one. Be creative, this is one place to just go for it. Rasp or file the handle to its profile shape.

Rasp or file the handle into its finished shape. This type of handle is more or less rounded all around. It fits into the natural curve of the palm and is surprisingly comfortable for shooting off the hand.

Once the shape is roughed down, sand it smooth, removing all tool marks.

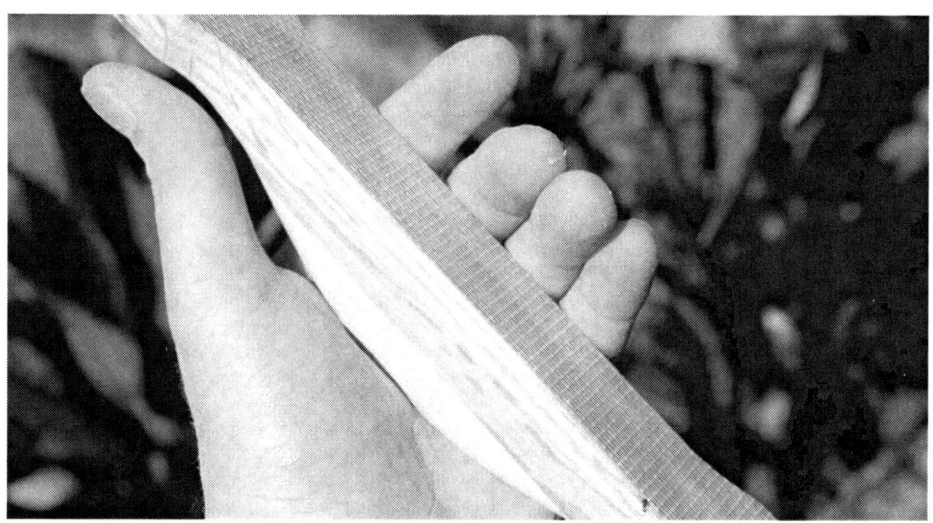

Here you can see how sharp the edges along the back of the bow are. Since the riser is glued on, it has a good chance of popping off if the handle bends. Since we tillered the bow to have a stiff handle, that won't be a big problem, but taking off too much from the main handle may start it bending.

The Backyard Bowyer

To prevent any major bend in the handle, round the handle just slightly, but not enough to drastically change the shape or weaken it.

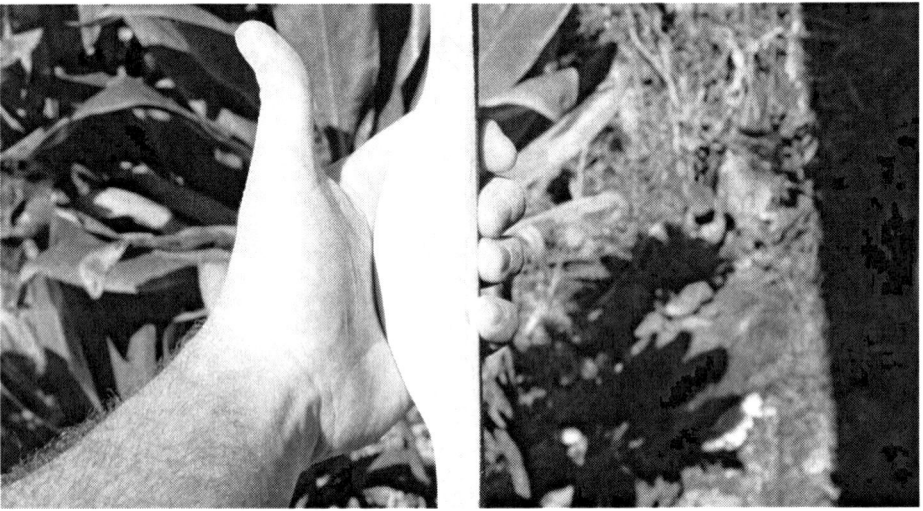

The handle should be comfortable and not digging into your hand when you hold it. Notice how the fades thin down into the actual bow wood, and not just in the handle riser. This will keep the handle from popping off, but even if it starts to come apart, a simple wrap will keep it in place.

Tip overlays serve to protect the bow's nocks as well as give the string a more solid purchase on the bow without cutting into the bow itself, which may weaken it at the tips.

Starting at the point where the bottom of the string groove ends, mark a line just steep enough to flatten the tip so the overlay can be glued on.

Flat Bow

The Backyard Bowyer

The tip overlays themselves can be anything, but very dense wood, bone and horn are good options. These are purpleheart, which is a very hard wood. I cut my overlays to three quarters of an inch by one and quarter inches, and they are about a quarter of an inch thick. Just as long as they cover the tip, size doesn't really matter.

The tip and overlay side by side.

Following your line, rasp or file the tip of the bow down flat.

Glue the overlay onto the back of the bow, lining it up so that most of the material sits where the string groove will come over the top of the nock.

Clamp the tip, and repeat on the other end.

The Backyard Bowyer

Let both tips dry for at least an hour. Overnight would be better, but an hour is enough.

Once dry, flatten any overhanging parts of the tip. Files are great for working on the bow tips.

You can either keep the stringer groove on the tip or remove it. Either way, start shaping down the tip and overlay to the shape of your choice. This traditional style tip is a good place to start.

Once the tip has been shaped, use a rat tail file or knife to continue the string nock across the top of the overlay.

The Backyard Bowyer

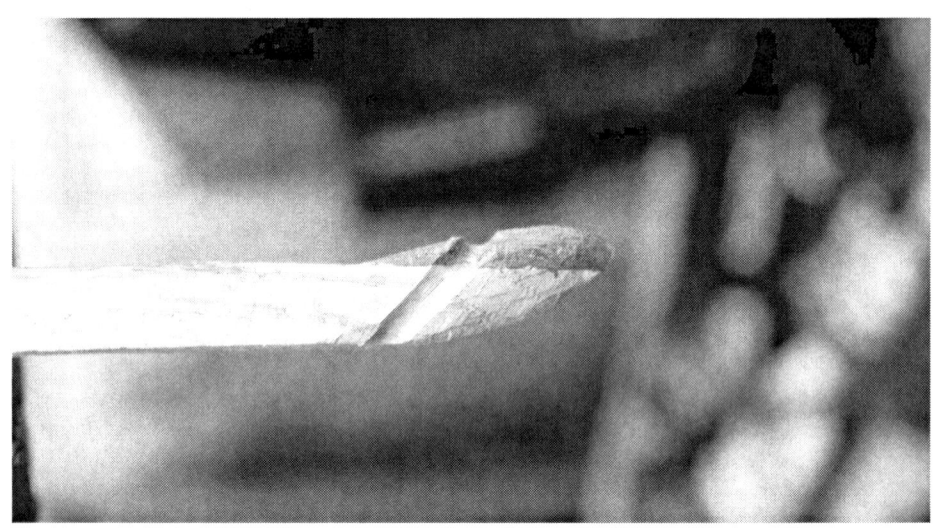

Here it is from the side.

The top.

And bottom.

Sand the tip down smooth, as well as the rest of the bow's limbs. Slightly round the back and belly just to keep splinters from raising in the long run.

Flat Bow

The Backyard Bowyer

Only a little rounding is necessary. Also sand the bow down smooth, going up the grits to about 400. This will be your finish sand.

There are many possible finishes for your bow. I like to use white petrolatum (petroleum jelly), though it must be rubbed into the bow every month or so, and any time the bow gets wet or exposed to moisture. Another option would be to finish the bow with a paint-on or spray on polyurethane or any other flexible sealing finish.

I prefer mineral oil and petroleum jelly as they just wipe on. They also go on and refinish very easily as opposed to other finishes that require sanding to fix or reapply. It also leaves the possibility of a more permanent finish in the future.

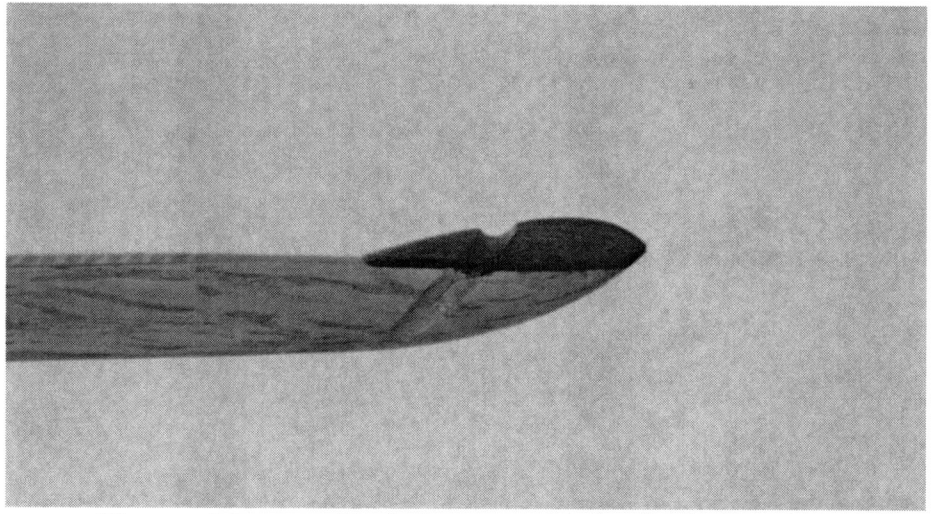

The purpleheart really darkens up with the finish. Petroleum jelly and mineral oil both lend a very natural finish to wood.

The Backyard Bowyer

Look at the figure in the maple. When looking for boards for building bows, keep an eye out for pieces like this. Someone had actually cut it off of a maple board and it was in a scrap bin at the hardware store.

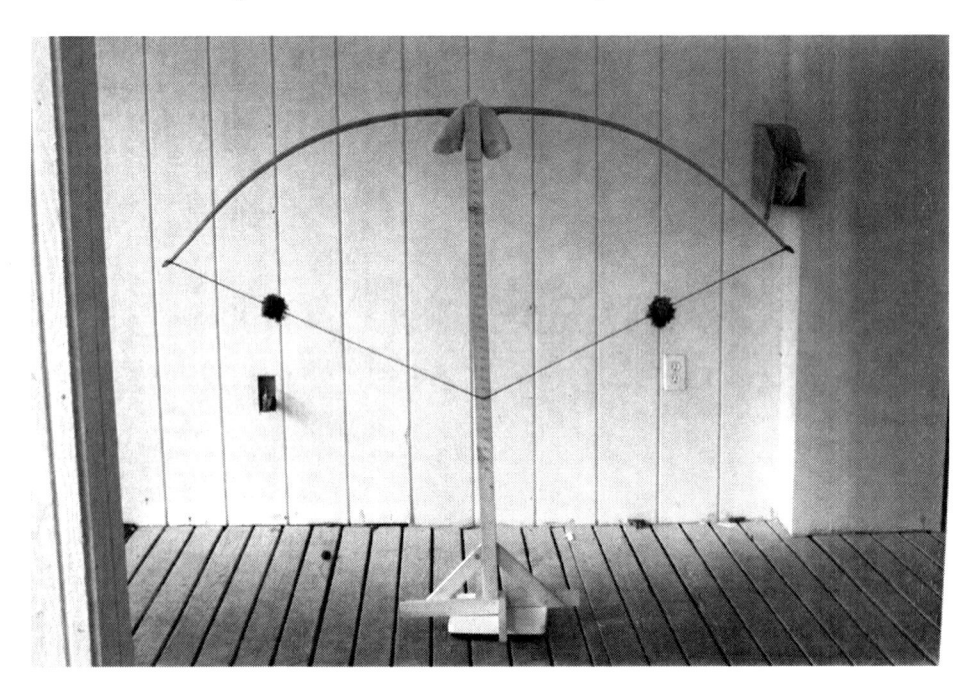

Now that the bow is finished, and after it has been broken in, weigh it one last time.

Mark the final weight on your bow, and be sure to sign it. It would also be a good idea to give your bow a name. I named this bow Trinity, more or less because of the three woods; red oak, maple, and purpleheart.

You're done! Congratulations on building a flat bow!

The Backyard Bowyer

Long Bow

One of the most influential bows in the world is the longbow, also known as the English Longbow. The most iconic type of English longbows would have to be a yew longbow with horn nocks. Yew, with its dense heartwood and elastic sapwood makes a good candidate for the highly stressed back and belly of the English longbow, and its horn nocks help keep the string from cutting into the nocks of the soft yew sapwood.

Yew aside, there are many woods that perform well in the form of an English longbow, but most woods will work in this shape, though performance is not exactly top. Then again, performance is not everything. I have never made an English style longbow that wasn't extremely fun to shoot with a smooth, sweet draw and snappy release, albeit with a slower arrow speed.

My fifth bow was a long bow, with flat back and rounded belly. It was very quick to make, tillered as if by itself, and has little problems. Even though its been abused and overdrawn almost regularly, it's still alive even after all this time without breaking or chrysaling. This bow is a little more straightforward than the flat bow. We'll even go over making nocks almost like the English longbows of old.

1-Design – Design considerations and the 5/8 rule.

2-Selecting Wood – Selecting a board that doesn't need a backing.

3-Roughing the Bow – Shaping the bow and rounding the belly.

4-Tillering – Bringing the bow up to its full draw and weight.

5-Finishing – Sanding, adding nocks, and sealing out moisture.

Design

The English longbow is perhaps the most famous and easily recognized bow in the world. It is also perhaps the simplest and most intuitive bow designs around (horn nocks aside). If the flat bow is simple in regards to basic geometric shapes, the English long bow, or longbow, is simple in regards to natural shape and form. While there are many design variations, (and even a standardized formula for modern English Longbows) all English longbows seems to follow a natural rounded shape.

Graceful in its own way, the longbow was developed primarily for war. Like most military weapons it is very straightforward and designed for raw power, distance, and ease of manufacture. The wood of choice for old English bows would have been Yew, a softwood with a few properties that make it ideal for the rounded longbow. Yet it's not the only ideal wood. Many hardwoods, especially dense tropical hardwoods, work better in the long, narrow longbow than the wide flatbow, and almost all hardwoods will work (though there are exceptions).

When dealing with English longbows, there are a couple designs to consider. Like most weapons of war, there were many variations between weapons of one type, and it wasn't until recently that the English bow has been "standardized". The British Longbow Society has set forth a rule defining what an English longbow is. This is the 5/8 rule, in which at any point on the bow, the bow's thickness is 5/8 its width. This means a section of limb that is one inch wide must be 5/8 of an inch thick. This is one option for building a bow, especially if you intend to participate in their competitions or similar English longbow competitions.

There are a couple styles that I often use regarding bow shape. The first is what I like to call the warbow style. Like the full flat bow, it is full width for most of the bow's length, sloping down to the tips of the bow from about three fourths down each limb. This style is very powerful, and for most woods besides yew or osage, I would suggest not fully rounding the belly, as the stress usually causes chrysals.

The Backyard Bowyer

In this style, more weight can be had by leaving the bow almost full thickness and width of a 1x2 board, and 80 inches long with three quarter of an inch wide tips. A bow like this made from red oak lumber can safely exceed 70 pounds of pull, which is impressive for an eight dollar board. Depending on the type of wood you are using, your results will vary, but if you want a heavy weight bow for target practice and hunting (a great feat with such a long bow), this is how you'd do it with board stock. At 72 inches, this style would safely handle 55 pounds.

The second is what I call the longbow style, which looks like the half-pyramid. The bow tapers in thickness and width evenly down its length, allowing for a very graceful bow that almost needs no tillering after rough shaping. This is the simplest way to go about building a longbow.

Regarding rounding the belly and back of the bow, I would not suggest rounding the back on a board bow without a very good backing, though a slight rounding of the edges is fine, and actually a very good idea. As for rounding the belly, woods like red oak, maple, ash, and other dense woods hold up fairly well to fully rounded bellies, especially in lower weights. Poplar, some birches, and most softwoods will simply collapse with rounded bellies. For these woods, slightly rounding the belly on the edges will work, and there is nothing that says an English longbow can't be shaped in this way.

Even spruce can be made to these dimensions, though 25 to 30 pounds is about as much weight as you will get from these bows. One way to get more poundage from spruce is demonstrated in one of my favorite fun bows. It's a 60 pound longbow I call Bruce.

Bruce is made of two fully-tillered spruce longbows, each pulling thirty pounds, and overall it is only rounded slightly to make it easier to grasp. Lashed together, they make one sixty pound bow. It's loud enough and creaky enough to send even deaf game running for the hills, but it's a fun bow to shoot, and even more fun to show off as it only cost two dollars to build.

When it comes to handles, most longbows have working handles, though non-bending handles are a possibility. If gluing on a handle, be sure to wrap it as some part of the handle will bend (unless the bow is made very thin).

Nocks are an interesting point with longbows. Most old English longbows had horn nocks. These were important for protecting the soft sapwood of yew. Any style of nock will work, though there is something about traditional horn nocks that is... awesome. If you haven't noticed by now, I'm not a very traditional person, so most of my 'horn' nocks have been made by laminating wood, bone, horn, antler, or plastic onto the tips of the bow and shaping them to look like horn nocks. I'll show how to make some simple ones in the chapter.

With longbows, length is fairly important. Unlike the flat bow we built in the last chapter, seventy inches is not excessively long. In fact, seventy inches is right about baseline for a 28 inch draw. This is probably why these bows are called longbows. They aren't exactly short. For every inch of draw up or down, increase or decrease the length of the bow by two inches. Or just make the bow longer, as there is nothing wrong, in my opinion, with a long bow.

The bow we will be doing is very straightforward. It will start with a six foot long board and will be 70 inches nock to nock. It will follow the 5/8 rule and be of the longbow style. It will also be fully rounded on the belly, though not rounding it fully would increase the poundage slightly. Without further delay, let's get started!

The Backyard Bowyer

Selecting Wood

This rift-sawn board has very straight grain, and the growth rings run evenly across the board end to end. This type of board can be used without a backing, though the bow should be fairly long and weights above fifty are pushing it.

Without a backing, look for no run-off in the grain of the board.

Roughing the Bow

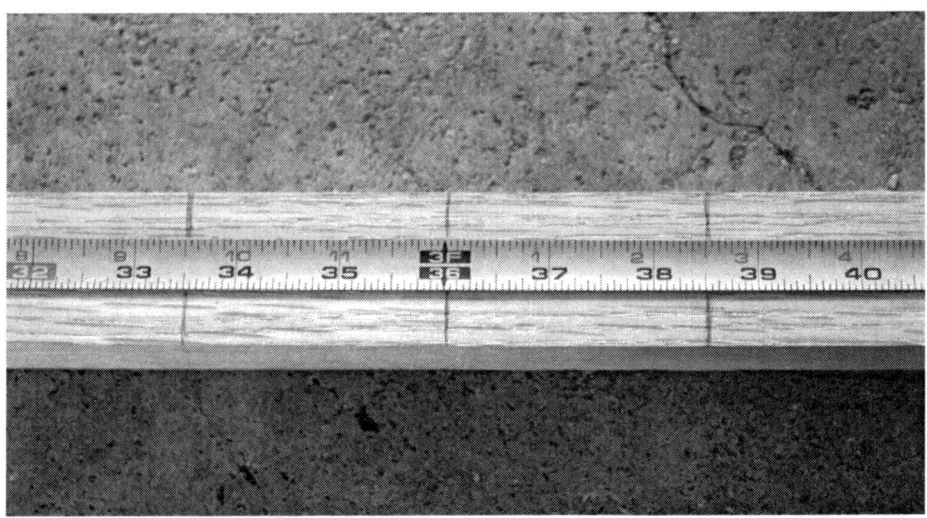

Just like the flat bow, measure center and 2.5 inches from the center on both sides. With this bow, more weight can be obtained safely by making the bow longer. 70 inches from nock to nock is a good distance to start. Most bows this length will end up around 40 pounds or so.

Long Bow

The Backyard Bowyer

Measure one and a quarter inches in width, and mark this line across the handle. Also mark the center of the handle like in the picture.

Place the stave on a chair, or like in this picture, the tiller.

Drape a string with a weight tied on either end, or clamp one end to the center of one end and hold the line taut. It is easier to adjust the string if one end isn't clamped, though.

Here the string lines up from the center of one end to the center of the other end. You can see the warp in the board.

Here you can see the line isn't centered.

Long Bow 113

The Backyard Bowyer

Adjust the ends until the string lines up from end to end through the center of the handle.

See how the new center is to the left of the measured center. A bow this long would not be affected by this war as much as a shorter bow, but it is still a good idea to center it.

The other end.

Mark the new center on both ends of the stave.

Long Bow 115

The Backyard Bowyer

mark and measure one inch in and half an inch wide at the end of the stave, which will become the bow's tip.

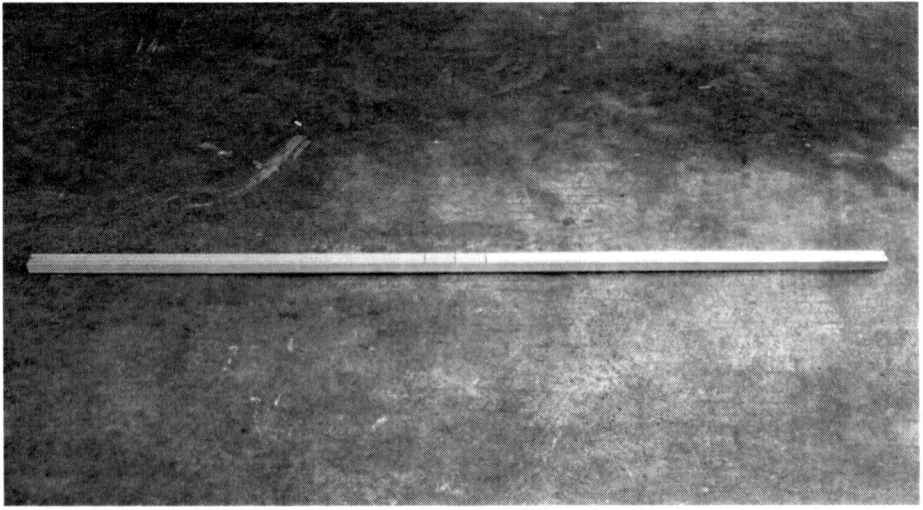

Using a straightedge, draw a line from the outside of the handle to the tip on each limb. Make sure the line starts at the point where the inside line of the handle is, not the outer edge.

Cut down to the lines. A draw knife or a large knife/machete makes this job very quick. Be sure to go light, taking a little off in many strokes, instead of one big stroke, as the wood can lift in huge chunks. Pressing too hard on the blade could snap it, so be gentle. Be sure to keep your fingers off the edge, and be very careful as any jerky movements could cause the blade to slip.

Once the rough shape is cut, shave down to the lines with the

The Backyard Bowyer

Surform®.

Once the shape is cut out, we will lay out the profile dimensions. In order for the bow to fit the 5:8, the handle should be about three fourths of an inch thick, which it should be if the board is a 1x2. The tips should be about three eighths of an inch thick.

Mark three eights of an inch at the tips.

118

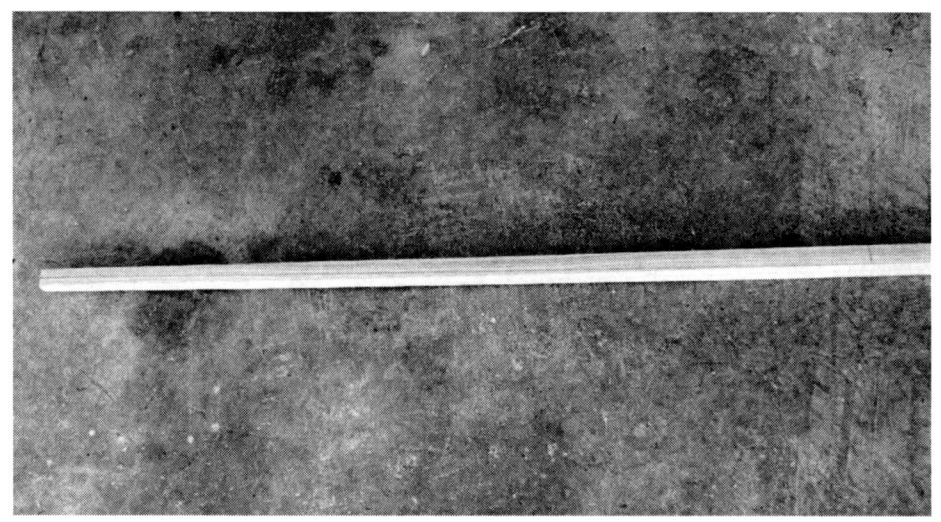

Using a straightedge, draw a line from the handle to the tip. Repeat this on all four sides.

Here's a better view of the line.

Long Bow 119

The Backyard Bowyer

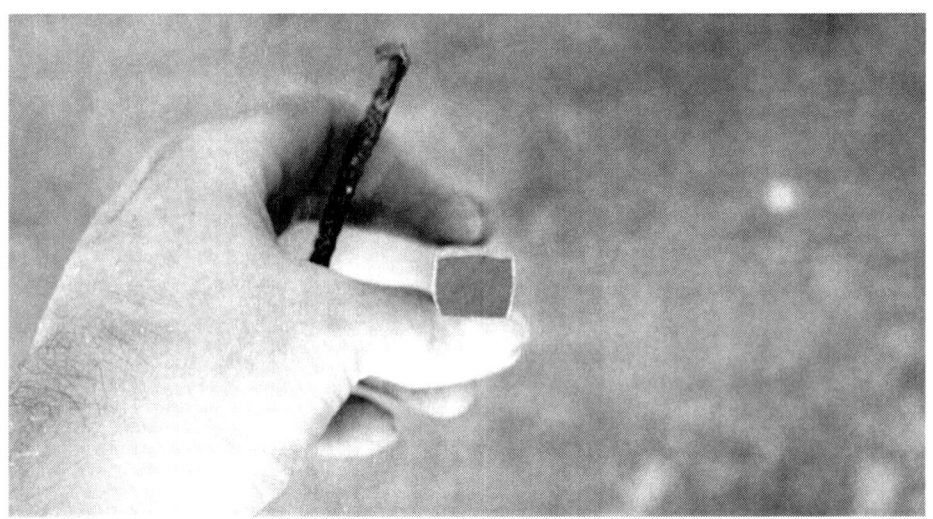

Once the thickness is roughed out, use the Surform® or a rasp to give the belly a rounded shape.

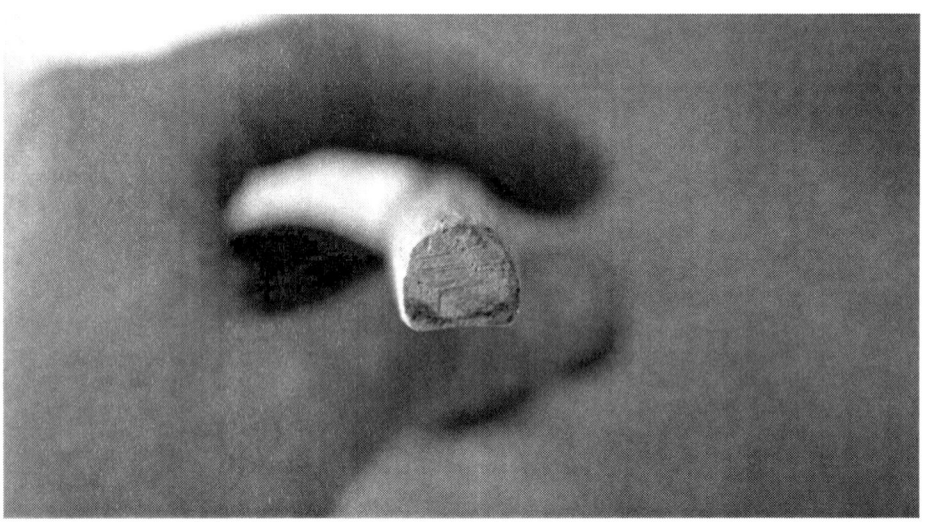

It should look like this, with half the width of the back of the belly rounded. By this I mean that at the tip, where the width is half an inch, round off only a quarter of an inch. This remaining full width area will help bring the bow into a good tiller once the bow starts bending.

Here's the belly rounded.

A better view. See how the curve runs smoothly down the whole limb.

Long Bow

Tillering

With a file, cut 45 degree notches from an inch down the back to about an inch an a half down the belly.

Here's a side view. File towards the center of the belly as well, which will help the string loop track in the nock and keep it from slipping off the bow when strung.

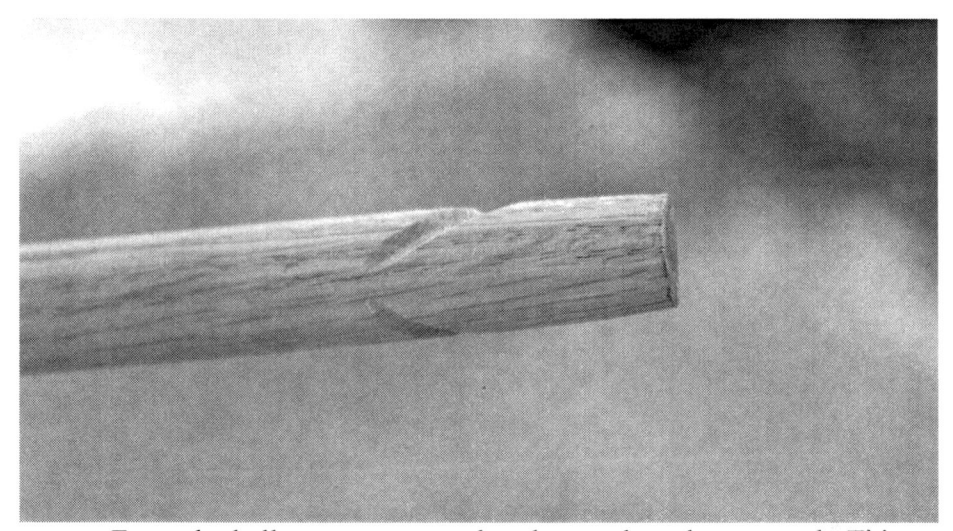

From the belly, you can see that the notches almost touch. This bottom area of the nock doesn't need to be as deep.

With the long string, get the bow bending about an inch or so. I don't find floor tillering necessary as the bow should be bending at these dimensions. Tillering the long bow goes much faster, as the bow bends its entire length, and is under very little stress at full draw. This bow can accommodate 32 inch + draws very well.

The Backyard Bowyer

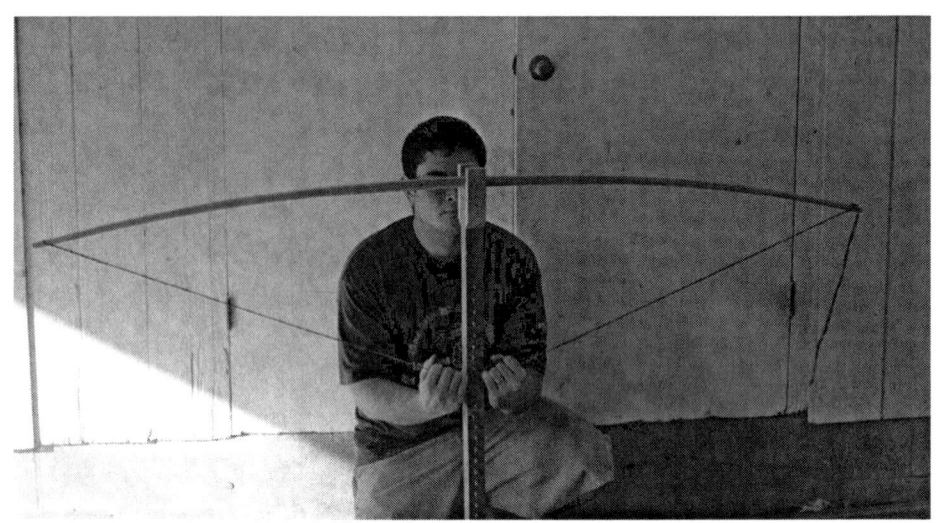

This is one way to exercise the limbs, and though it is a little more awkward, it prevents overdrawing because you have the tiller as a reference.

This is another method of exercising. It's much quicker, though you can overdraw the bow easily. Just take it slow and be patient.

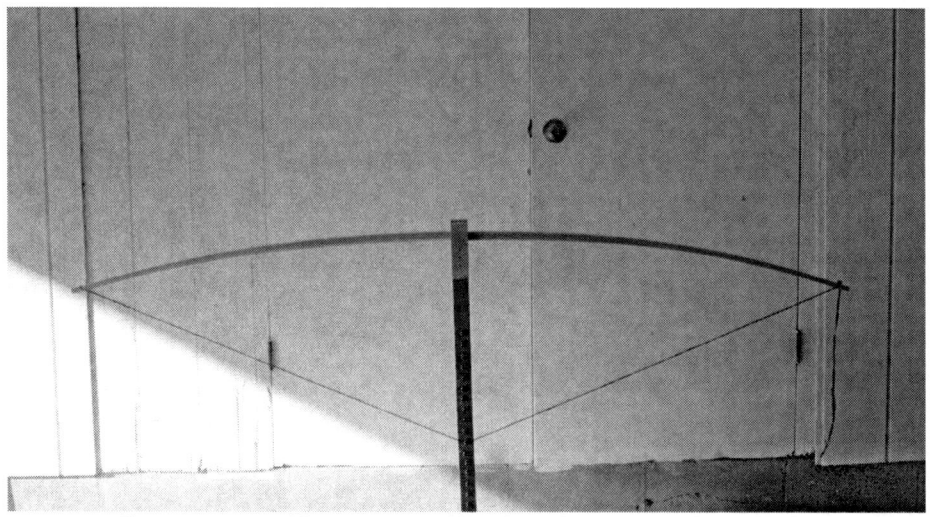

When uneven tiller appears like in this picture, fix it before going any further.

Here the bow is much more even. Minor adjustments are all that is needed unless another major flaw appears.

The Backyard Bowyer

Once the bow is tillered about halfway with the long string, shorten the string to no brace.

Once the bow is tillered up to 24 inches, shorten the string to half brace, which is about 3 inches of brace.

Once the bow has been tillered to 28 inches, shorten the string to full brace, and give it another tiller check.

Here's the bow, with final string, at 28 inches. From here be sure to break the bow in. Leaving the bow strung overnight helps to get the bow used to flexing, though sometimes it will increase string follow, especially if the area you live in is humid.

Long Bow 127

The Backyard Bowyer

Finishing

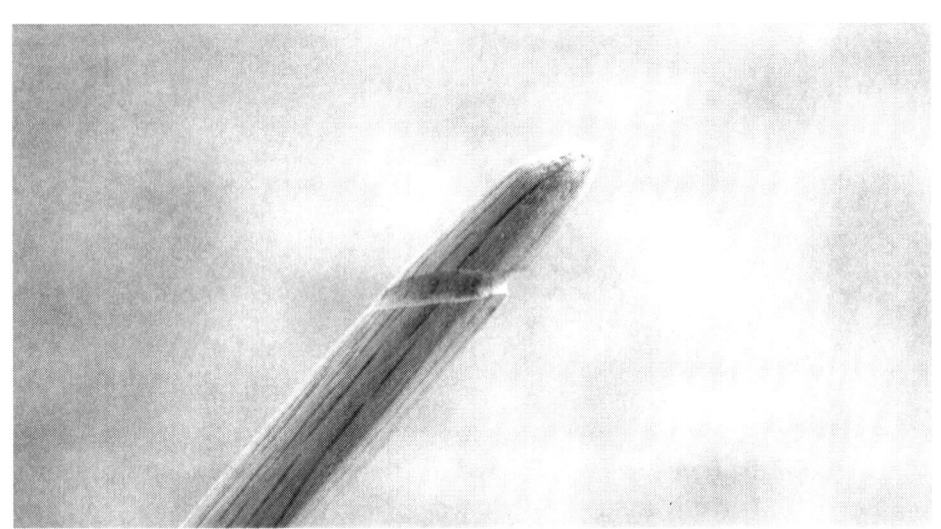

Now that the bow is broken in, you could simply sand down the nocks, shaping them like this, and consider yourself done. Though, it just wouldn't feel like an English Longbow without added nocks, whether they be horn or not.

Any wood will work for these tips, bone and horn work especially well. These will sit on top of the nock, instead of being secured over it like traditional horn nocks. Three quarter by three quarter inch by about two and a half inches is a good rough measure for your tip pieces.

Mark a line that runs at a shallow angle down the tip.

Shave the back side of the nock down to that line, then sand both the overlay and the nock.

The Backyard Bowyer

Glue and clamp the tip in place until it dries. If your glued on nocks extend past the bow itself when finished, like the top nock of this bow will be, let the glue dry overnight. Otherwise, an hour is fine.

It's a good idea to sketch out what the nock will look like so you have something to go by. The large overlay allows for a nock that resembles a horn or antler nock in shape.

Form the nock. I find it helps to use the surform to rough the general shape, then get the inside contours with a half round file. With the rat tail file, follow the existing string grooves up and over the nock. With a thick nock like this, it is possible to make the top groove very deep, which will keep the string from accidentally slipping off.

Here's the top of the nock.

Long Bow 131

The Backyard Bowyer

And here's the bottom.

Just like the top nock, sketch out the design of the bottom nock. I prefer the more rounded style of nock for the bottom because it's less likely to catch on things and break as a pointed and hooked nock, especially because these are made of wood. It's also easier to string the bow either with or without a stringer when the bottom nock is rounded.

Once shaped, here is the finished bottom nock from the side.

Here it is from the top.

Long Bow 133

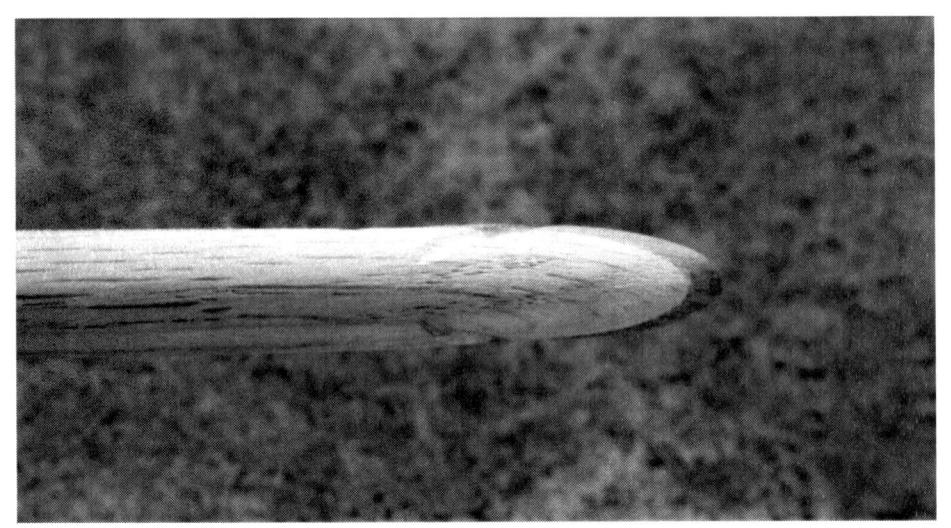

The Backyard Bowyer

Here it is from the bottom.

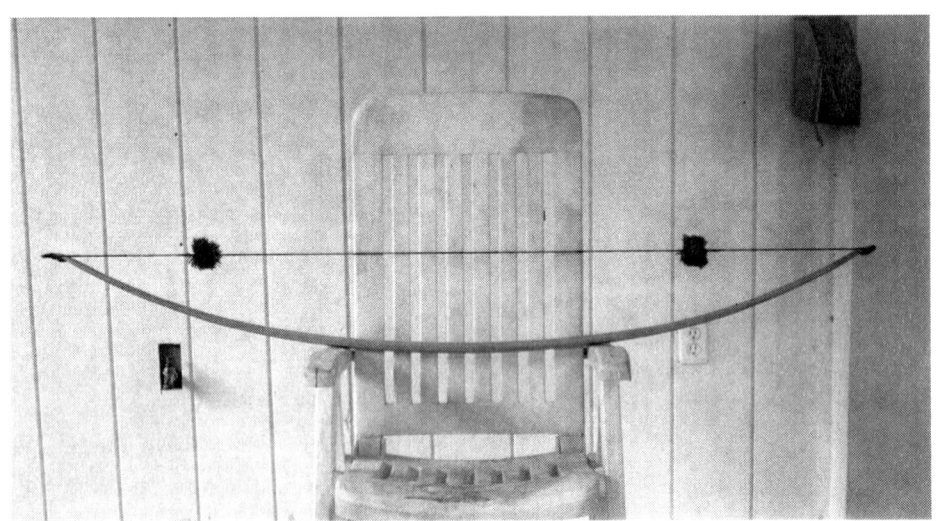

    Once the nocks are finished and sanded, sand the entire bow, making sure to no take off too much. Especially on a bow without a backing, make sure to sand as high a grit as possible on the back. Once sanded, finish the bow with a finish of your choice.

Here's the bow finished and drawn.

Now of course, this is an English longbow! You can't be all boring! It's an English longbow! Go find a nice open field or an archery range with wide open spaces, and let those arrows fly!

The Backyard Bowyer

Handle Wrap and Arrow Rest

One of the simplest ways to increase handle comfort and improve your accuracy is to wrap the handle and attach an arrow rest. A simple handle wrap can help with indexing. It creates a place to put your hand constantly every time, allowing you to differentiate top and bottom limbs, as well as knowing where to place the arrow. All of this helps to increase your accuracy with your bow by eliminating extra variables.

An arrow rest serves the dual purpose of not only giving a consistent arrow placement on the bow, but also by getting the arrow off the hand.

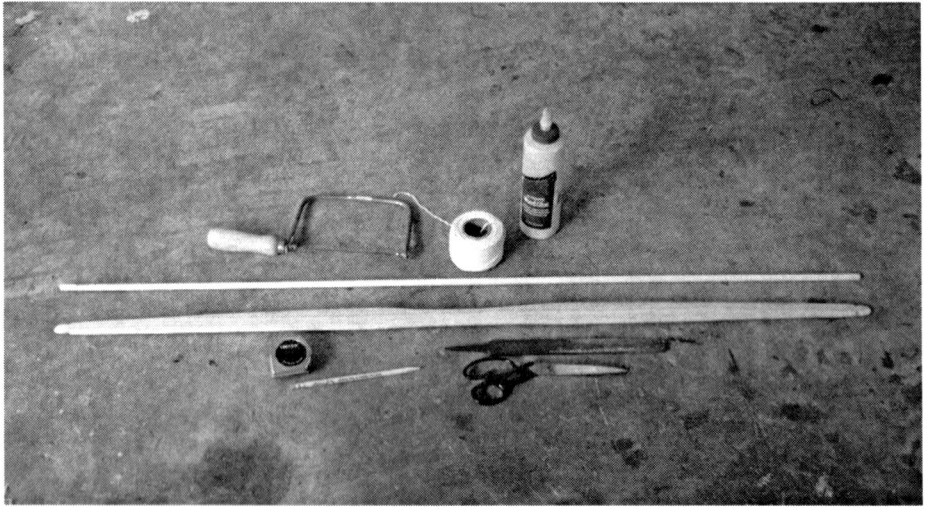

Gather your materials. For the arrow rest, a dowel works well. The dowel should have a diameter that is the same or a little smaller than the thickness of your main handle section. For bows with raised risers, the thickness right at the fades is a good measure. A saw, tape measure, file, sandpaper, and a pair of scissors are all you need.

As for the wrap itself, any string will work. Leather, cotton, hemp, nylon, jute, and other string works fine. It's really up you. Cotton and leather add comfort as compared to hemp or jute, which becomes rather scratchy once glued down.

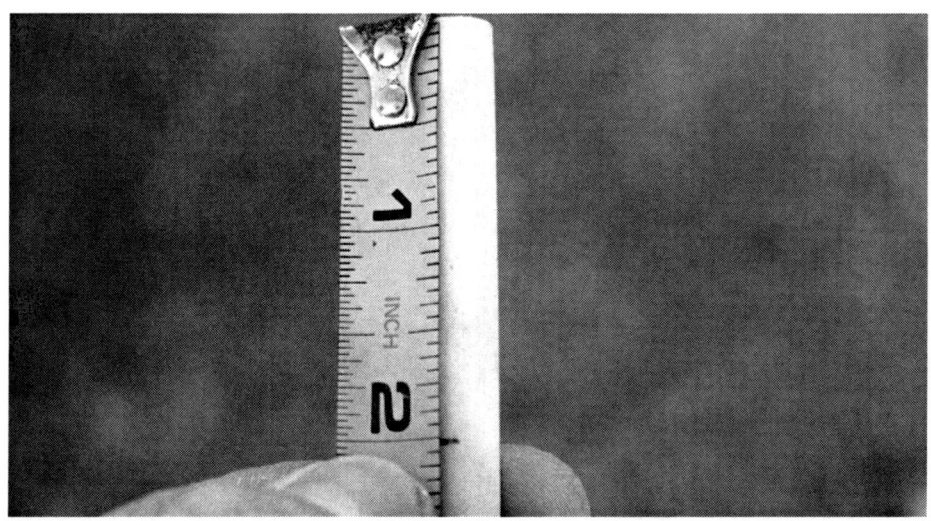

Measure two inches down the end of the dowel. Anywhere from one to two inches is good for the arrow rest, though it can be made shorter. The longer the rest, the wider the handle will be once the wrap is finished. A short rest may not wrap very well.

The Backyard Bowyer

Mark a line that runs along the grain on one end. This is where you'll split the dowel piece.

Split the piece in half, then sand it to bring it down to halfway.

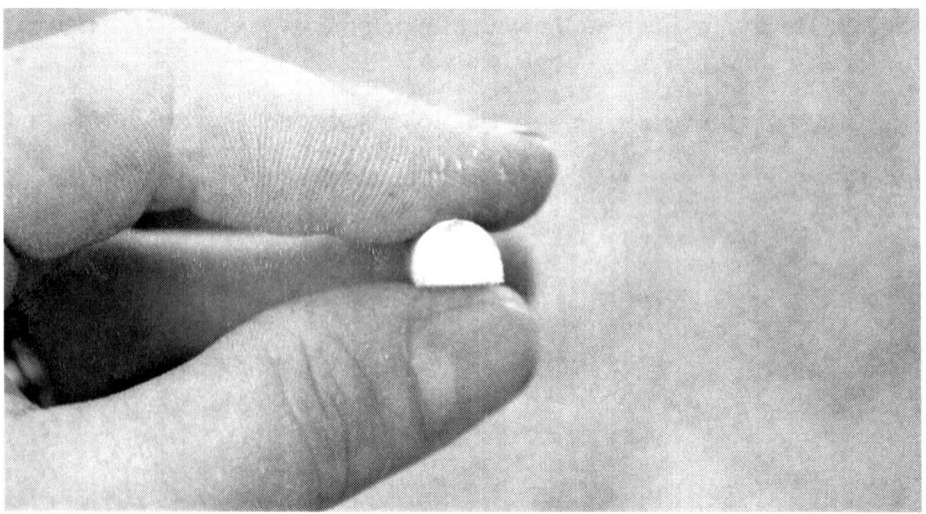

Here is the end of the piece. The dowel was not perfectly round, but you can see the flat edge on the bottom.

138

Using a rasp or sandpaper, flatten the dowel at an angle, leaving the curved part untouched.

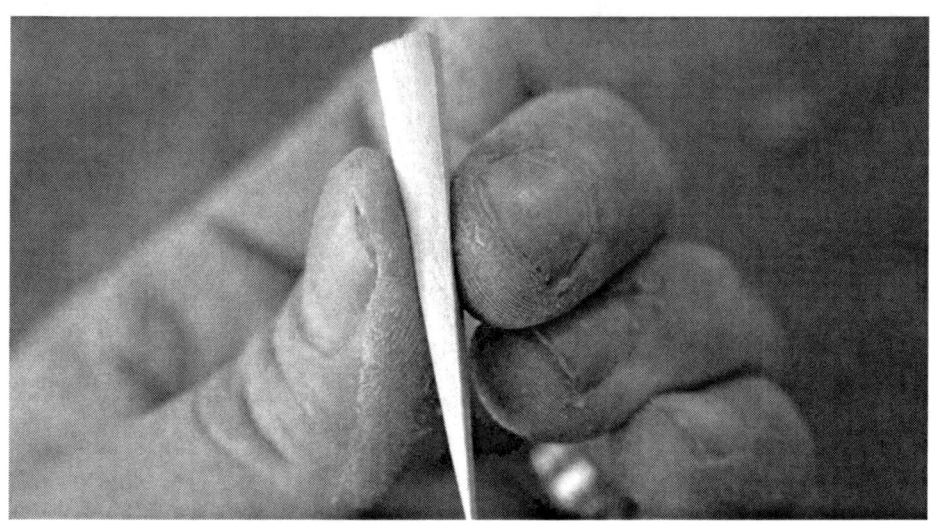

Here's a better view of the taper.

Handle Wrap and Arrow Rest

The Backyard Bowyer

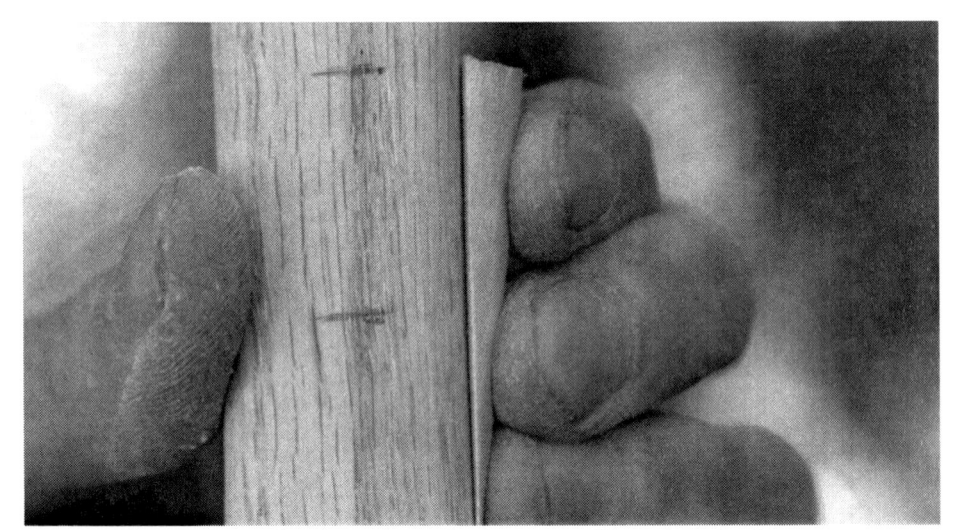

If you place the dowel on the bow, you'll notice (unless your handle is flat on the side) that the dowel doesn't sit well on the handle. To fix this, we'll sand the inside of it to get the same contour as the handle.

Starting with a low 60-80 grit of sandpaper, wrap the paper around the handle with the rough side facing out. With small, quick stroke, run the dowel against the paper, as if trying to get it to stick to the side of the handle. This creates an inside curve on the dowel.

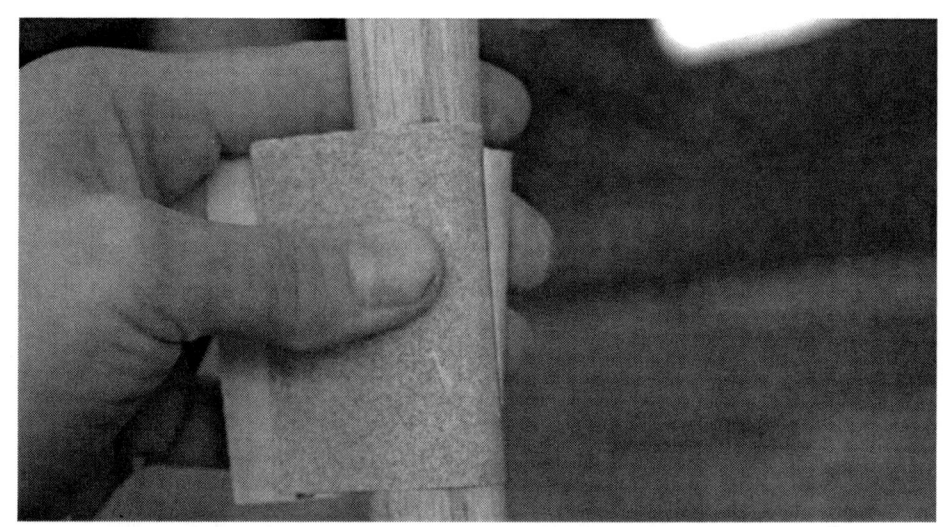

Once the main curve has been established, just clean it up with a finer 120-150 grit.

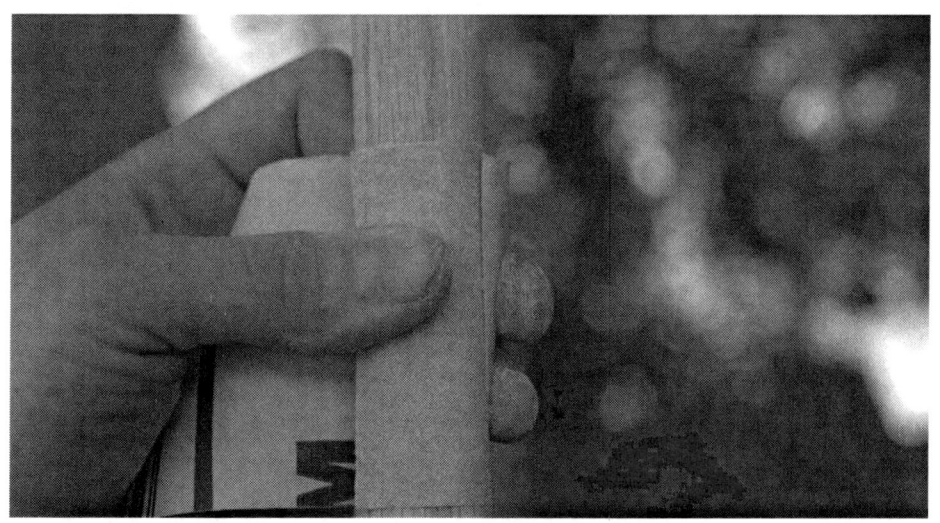

And finally finish with about a 220 grit.

Handle Wrap and Arrow Rest

The Backyard Bowyer

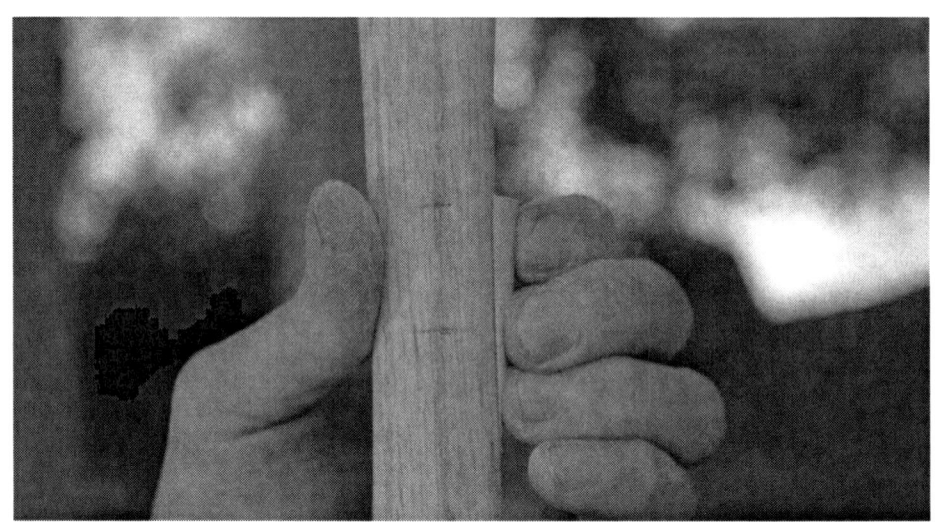

Now the arrow rest fits snugly against the side of the handle. The mark on the handle itself is where the top of your hand rests when shooting the bow, and where the rest will go. I like to mark this while breaking a bow in, so I know where the best place to put the rest is. You also want to file the top of the rest down so it's flat and not slanted.

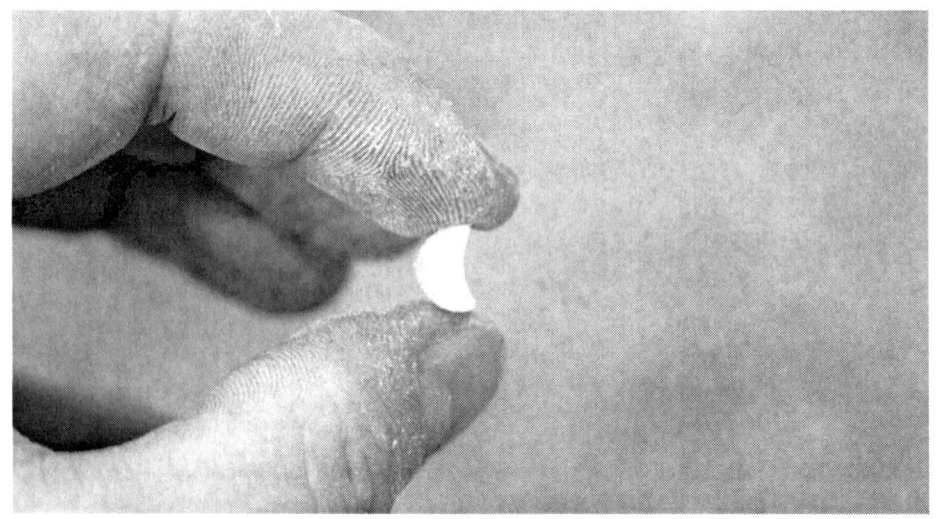

Here's the inside curve of the arrow rest. Most bow handles won't be as small in thickness and drastic in curve as this bow.

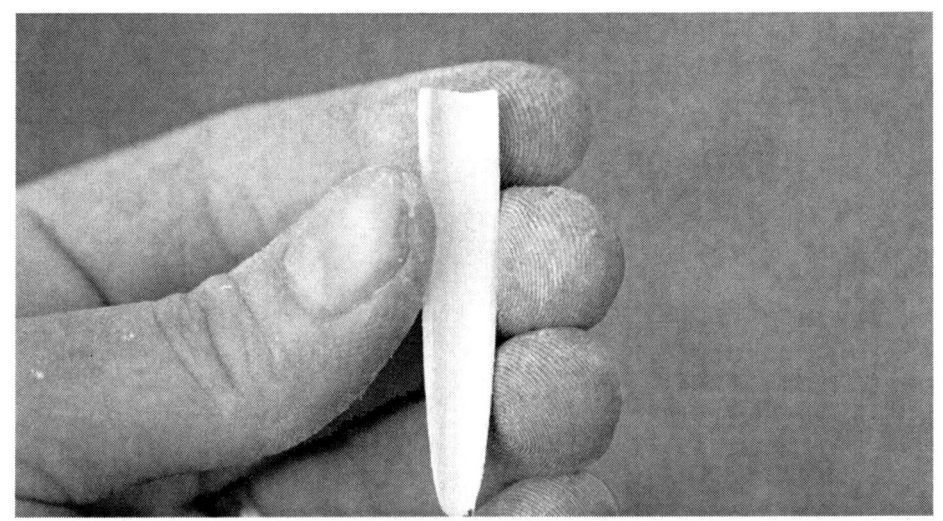

Wipe the inside of the arrow rest and the handle with a cloth dampened with water or alcohol to get rid of any fine wood dust.

Place a thin layer of glue on both sides and press together. If you don't want to wrap the handle, clamp it in place by either using a clamp, wrapping it with a cohesive bandage or tape, or tying the rest to the handle with twine. If you are going to wrap the handle, the wrapping will serve as a clamp.

Handle Wrap and Arrow Rest 143

The Backyard Bowyer

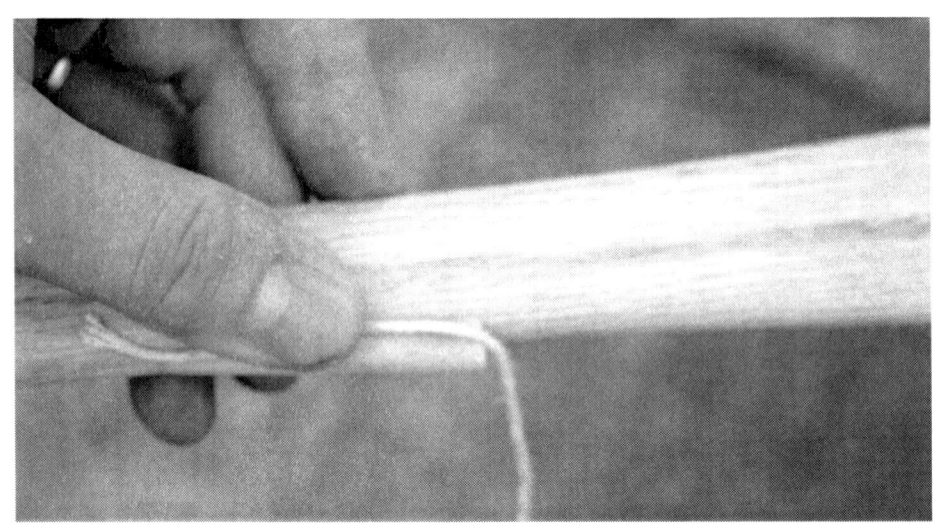

Begin the wrap by taking the loose end of your twine and holding it down the handle by about two inches.

Starting from the top, take the other end of the twine and wrap it tightly around the handle. The loose end tucked under the wrap will hold the top end together and keep it from unraveling. Once you reach about this point, twist the top of the wrap. If you go one way, the wrap will loosen and come off, but if you twist the other way, the wrap will tighten, but the very top, where the loose end goes under the wrap, will get loose. To tighten the wrap, pull down on the loose end that's showing under the wrap, and the top will be nice and secure.

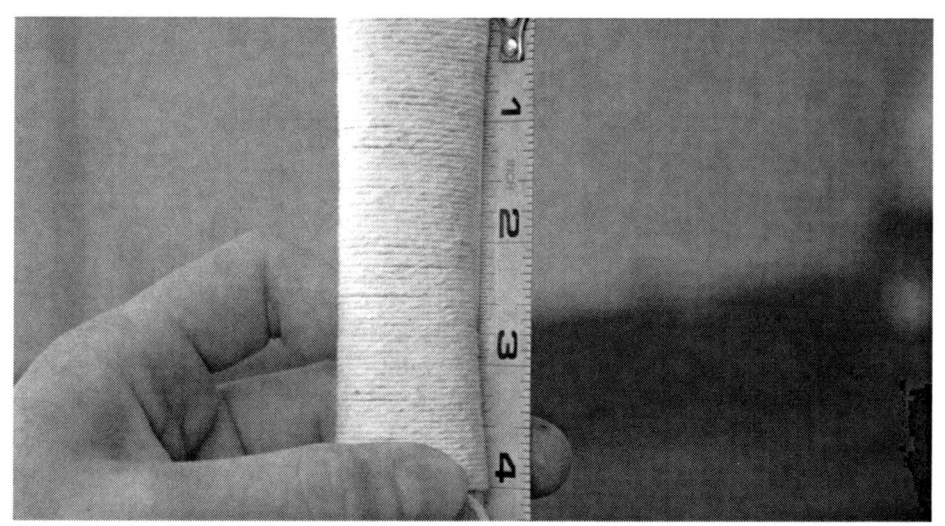

Continue wrapping until about half an inch before you want the wrap to end.

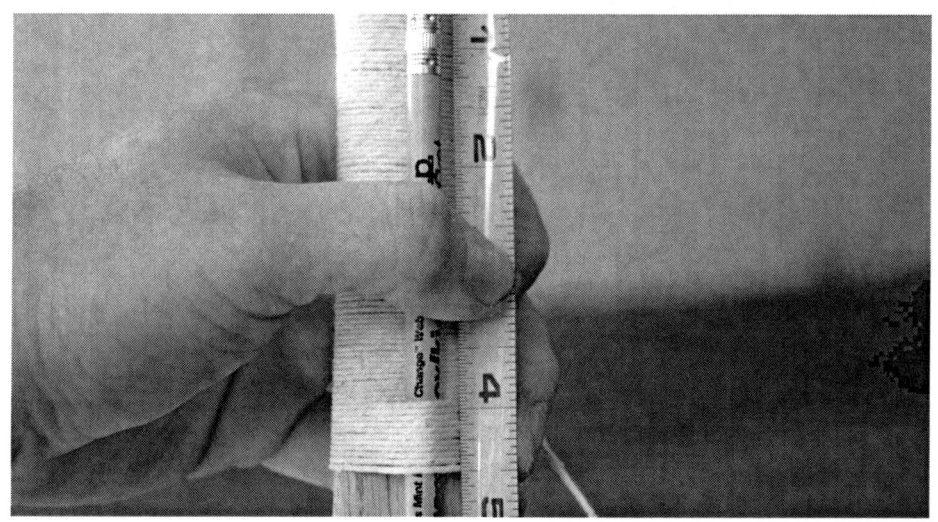

Place a pencil or other thin, smooth object on the handle and wrap

Handle Wrap and Arrow Rest 145

The Backyard Bowyer

over it for half an inch.

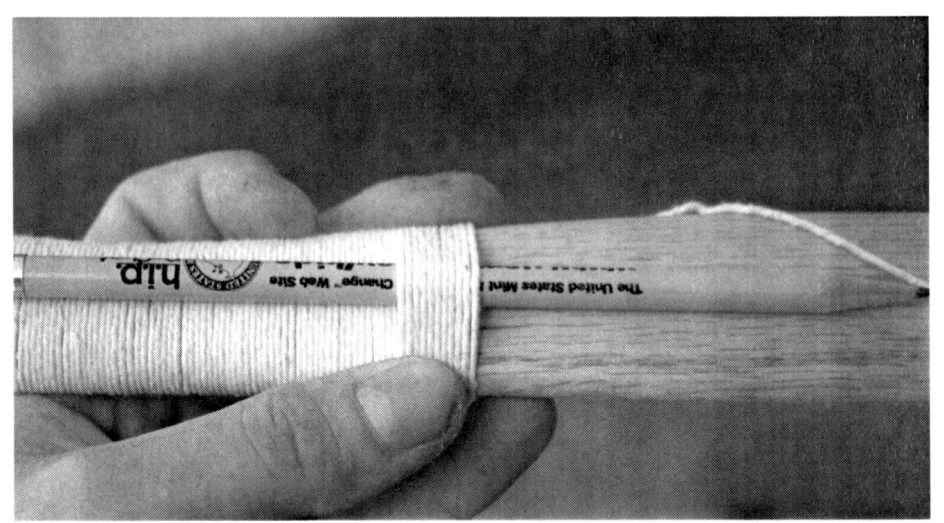

Cut the end of the twine, leaving a few inches to work with.

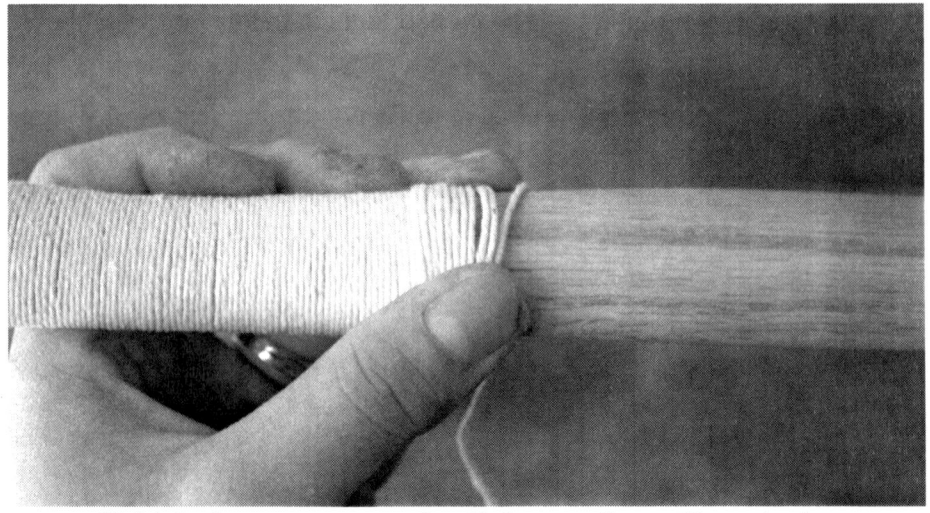

Hold the bottom wrap, and pull the pencil out. Keep the loops from closing up, and feed the end of the twine through them. This will lock the bottom of the wrap.

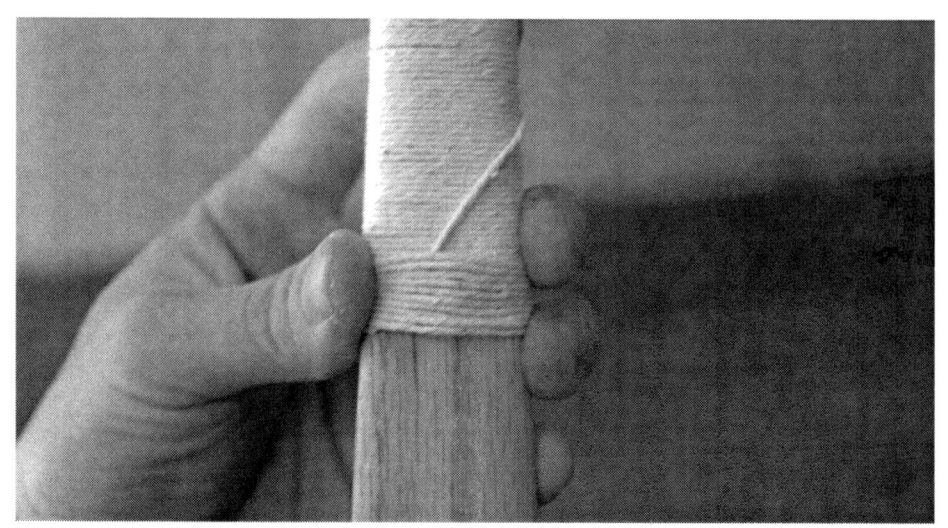

Once the end is pulled through, twist and tighten the bottom of the wrap just like the top, pulling on the loose end.

Once the wrap is tight, cut the end of the twine flush with the wrap, careful not to cut the wrap itself.

Handle Wrap and Arrow Rest

The Backyard Bowyer

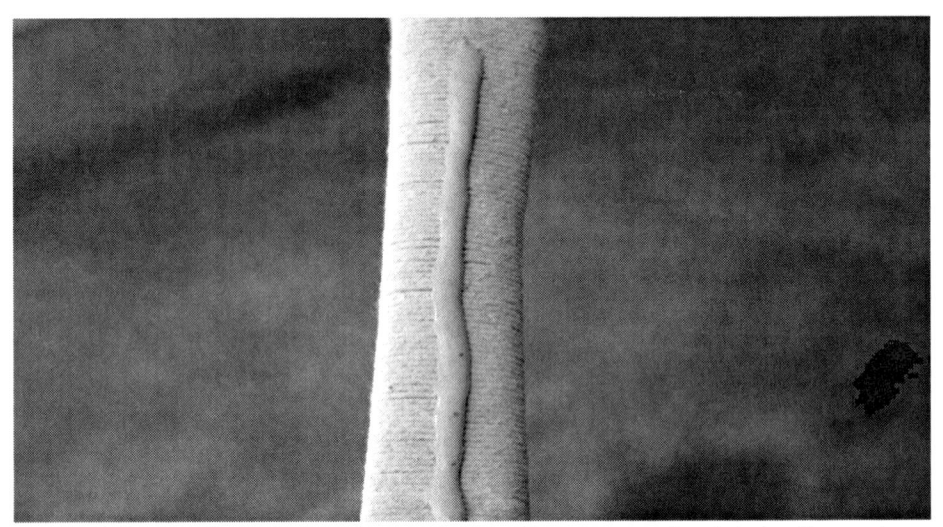

Place a line of glue down the handle wrap and rub it in. Repeat this until the glue has soaked through the twine completely. I like to use a waterproof wood glue mixed with a little bit of water.

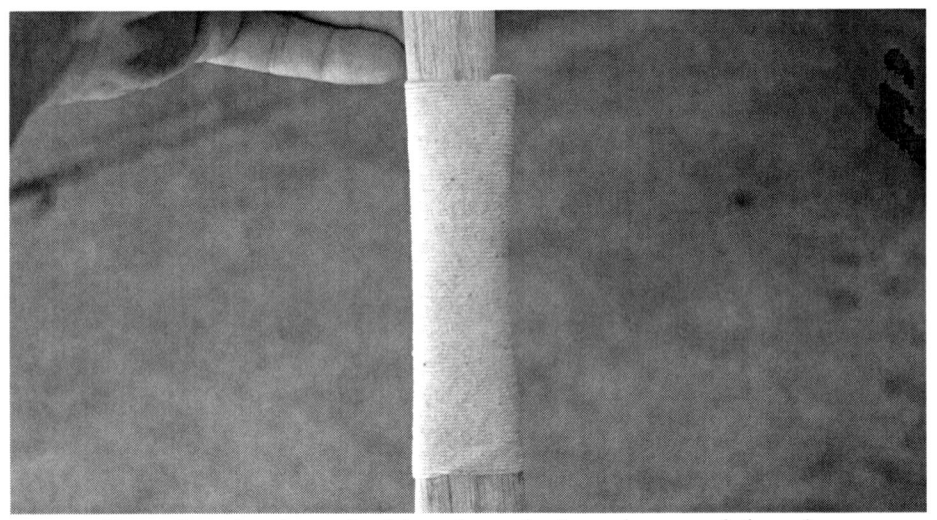

Once the glue is soaked in, place the bow in a cool dry place where it won't be disturbed and let it dry. I would let it dry overnight, but it should be dry enough to use in about an hour.

Here is the finished handle. You can see the handle is very wide near the rest and taper down. If that seems uncomfortable, you can make the rest shorter, or just don't taper the dowel and have the arrow rest run from the top to bottom so that the handle is even. As a side note, this method of gluing on an arrow rest also works for gluing on nocks for making glued-on pin nocks. Like this handle, those types of nocks should be wrapped, though thinner cord would work much better.

An alternative wrap would be to simply wrap a piece of leather around the handle section and lace it up with twine or leather lace like a shoe. Leather can also be glued on in layers to add an arrow shelf, and even build up the flat back of an English longbow or flat bow like in these pictures.

Handle Wrap and Arrow Rest 149

The Backyard Bowyer

Glossary

And that's it, congratulations on making your first (or second, third, fourth, three hundredth, etc.) bow! Here's a little glossary just to clear up any of the bizarre terms I may have used in the book.

AMO- The Archery Manufacturer & Merchants Organization is a group that sets the standards for the production of archery equipment. This allows all makers of archery equipment to be on the same page in reference to draw length, weight, and other defining points in the make and marketing of archery equipment. This organization, however, is now the ATA, or Archery Trade Association, though AMO as a form of standardization is still used.

Arrow- An arrow is the the projectile used with a bow. It consists of a shaft, which is the main body of the arrow, a point, which strikes the target, a nock, which contacts the string, and fletching that helps to stabilize the arrow in flight.

Back- The back of the bow is the part of the bow that faces away from you when shooting it. The tips bend away from this side when the bow is strung. This part of the bow is under tension, and needs to be able to stretch in order for the bow to work.

Backing- Anything placed on the back of a bow. It can be anything from wood, cloth, fiberglass, paper, glue, or even just air.

Belly- The belly of the bow is the side of the bow that faces toward you when shooting, and when strung, the tips bend toward this side. The belly of a bow has to be able to withstand the forces of compression, as the bow's bending will crush the belly wood slightly.

Bowyer- A person who makes bows.

Brace- The distance between the handle and string of a bow when it is strung. Full brace is usually around 6 inches.

British Longbow Society- A group formed to perpetuate the use of the English Longbow. They set the standards for most English

Longbow competitions regarding bow construction and shooting style.

Chrysal- Thin cracks on the belly of a bow that run perpendicular to the limbs. These are caused by the bow wood beginning to fail under compression.

Compound Bow- A bow that uses cams or pulleys. These bows are very accurate, and have very flat trajectories. Considered to be the pinnacle of archery technology.

Curly Grain- A type of figure in wood, curly grain is an undulation of wood fibers. It usually appears as sort of tiger stripes, and usually has the light reflecting quality (chatoyancy) similar to cat's eye gemstones. This type of figure presents exposed ends of wood fibers to the surface of the wood, weakening its ability to withstand tension.

Draw Length- The length that a bow is drawn to. Wooden bows are usually made for only one single draw length.

Draw Weight- A measure of how much force is required to pull a bow to a certain length of draw. Draw weight can be used to approximate the power of a bow, but some bows are more efficient than others.

Draw- The act of pulling back on the bowstring and consequently, the bow.

Early Growth- Wood that is quickly deposited early on in a tree's yearly growth cycle. It is usually spongy and weak compared to late growth.

Fades- The fades are the portion of bow next to a stiff handle riser that fades down into the bow's limbs. This is the transition between bow limbs and handle.

Figure- Any type of activity or irregularity in wood. Figure should be avoided on all-wood bow limbs.

Flat Bow- A type of bow that has wide, flat limbs that are thin compared to its width.

Frets- The same as chrysals.

Furring Strip- A 1x2 or 2x2 board of softwood used for reinforcing drywall and for framing in structures. Some common furring strip woods are spruce (often called whitewood), pine, and douglas fir.

Grain- The orientation of wood fibers as they radiate outward from the interior of a tree. Grain runs perpendicular to growth rings.

The Backyard Bowyer

Growth Ring- Layers of wood produced by a tree as it goes through its yearly cycle of growth. Growth rings run in circles radiating from the center of a tree. They run perpendicular to grain.

Handle- The section of bow that you grip with your hand. This is where the bow makes contact with you, and it is the main pivot point for the bow.

Heart Wood- Heart wood is the denser, more resinous interior of a tree. In most woods, heart wood is darker and dense, though usually more brittle than sap wood.

Knot- A knot is the evidence of a growth in the tree. If a branch or shoot is cut through, a knot forms. Knots are weak points for both the back and belly of a bow and should be avoided.

Lamination- A lamination is a glued bond. Two pieces of wood glued together as one is an example of a lamination.

Late Growth- Wood that is deposited slowly throughout the later part of a tree's growth cycle. It is usually more dense and tough than early growth.

Limb- A bow's limb is the part that bends and does work.

Longbow- A longbow is usually long, narrow, and thick compared to its width.

Machine- An object that does work, usually through the transfer or transformation of energy.

Nock- Any point that contacts the string when a bow is in use.

Recurve Bow- A type of bow that has limbs that are curved towards the back of the bow near the tips.

Riser- The handle section on a stiff handled bow. It is usually much thicker than the rest of the bow and includes the bow's grip and arrow rest or shelf.

Sap Wood- The less-dense, though more elastic outer wood that is found growing outside of the heart wood.

String- A string is used to place a bow under tension, draw the bow, and hold arrows.

Tiller- Basically, the curve of a bow during its stages of draw.

Disclaimer : Bows and arrows can be dangerous if used improperly. Never fire a bow in the direction of houses or in places where there is limited visibility. Always check and be sure of local laws regarding the use of bows and arrows. Never point a bow at another person, as they can cause serious harm or injury. Be sure of any laws regarding hunting or target practice and adhere to them for the safety of yourself and others.

Acknowledgments

I would like to thank everyone who has helped me to make this dream a reality.

My supportive wife Angie, whose stubborn attitude and encouraging words kept me on the path.

My parents Edwin and Dee Dee, who got me started, always supported me and continue still to give me the push I need when I most need it.

My brother Brian, who always figured I'd be a self-made success. Remember, no matter how old you get, I'll always be your little brother.

My friends, who are always there to lend a helping hand, foot, joke, or opinion. You guys know who you are.

I would also like to acknowledge my two camera guys.
Brandon Kamita, photos from pages 20-35.
Brendan Allard, photos from pages 64-88.
I personally took all the other photos and did the nifty illustrations of bows in the design sections.

Here are some organizations that have been mentioned in this book, as well as the information to one book that has helped me greatly in my understanding of bow construction and the sport of archery.

Archery Manufacturers and Merchants Organization, AMO, <http://www.amo-archery.org>
Archery Trade Association, ATA, <http://www.archerytrade.org>
British Longbow Society, BLBS, <http://www.askarts.co.uk/longbow.html>
Burke, Edmund H, *Archery Handbook*, ARCO Publishing Company, New York, NY, 1965
Stanley Hand Tools, Black and Decker, <http://stanleytools.com>

The Backyard Bowyer

Bonus Track

I personally love it when artists put an extra track at the end of an album. Usually it's something they normally wouldn't put in an album, something unfinished or something they don't think fits. Well that's the predicament I'm in with this chapter. I'm no expert on making strings or arrows, and when I'm building bows for other people, and even my own personal bows for hunting and target practice, I buy those things.

I do know that arrows are expensive, and strings can rack up the expense too, especially if you plan on building a lot of bows. I'd hate it if you bought this book, read it all, and decided to not build a bow because you don't want to buy a string and a set of arrows. I know I wouldn't. I'd rather make them myself.

While I know a thing or two about making a stick bend, arrows and strings are still rather elusive to me. My strings, when I do make them, are crude and not so pretty, but they work. My arrows, though they work, are not the highest performers out there. Since these aren't as premium as my bows, consider this section the Bonus Track! Enjoy!

The Magical Angler String

Of all the strings I've ever made, these are by far the quickest, easiest, and ugliest strings I've done. They are tough, don't easily slip off of bows, and require little maintenance, plus they are fairly inexpensive to make (the materials for a few strings can be had at Wallyworld for less than five bucks).

First step is to find some string material. The reason I call it the magical angler string is that the main material is braided fishing line. One of the best materials for traditional bowstrings is Dacron, and Dacron just so happens to be one of the types of fishing line available. Braided nylon fishing line, braided nylon leather stitching thread, and even store-bought Dacron bowstring material will all work for this type of string. Just make sure you start with 30-40 pound test/breaking strength on your individual strands.

I find that fourteen strands is more than enough for bows up to sixty pounds of pull, though theoretically, fourteen strands is enough for a hundred and ten pound bow. If you want to push the limits, multiply the weight of your bow by four or five, and divide that by the test of your line. That's how many strands you absolutely need. I find fourteen strands to give a nice, full string.

Now that you've got your material, cut out as many strands as you need, in the length of your bow's AMO measurement (nock to nock) plus eight inches. So for a 72 inch bow that's 70 inches between nocks, 78 inches per strand is a good place to start. Separate these into two bundles, making sure that they are even. So if your bow should have fifteen strands, round up. If you really want an odd number of strands, you can make three bundles, as the technique is the same, it just takes a little getting used to.

Bonus Track   155

The Backyard Bowyer

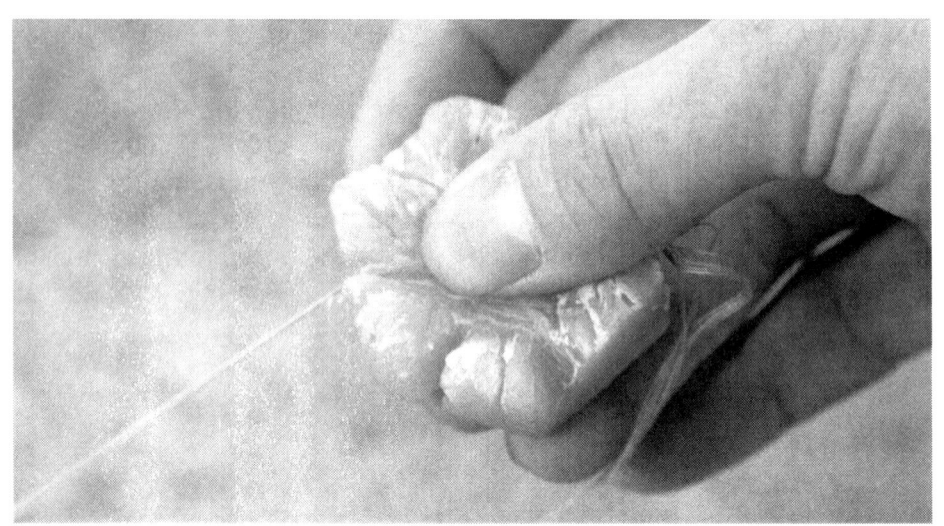

Next, take your bundles and run then through some wax like this. Any solid, sticky wax works. Beeswax is my favorite, as the finished strings smell like they are honey roasted. Candle wax (paraffin) works as well, though unscented candles make the string smell like gasoline. Just pull the strands through the wax enough to coat them, and then rub the bundles quickly with either your fingers or a smooth cloth (paper also works) to melt the wax into the strands.

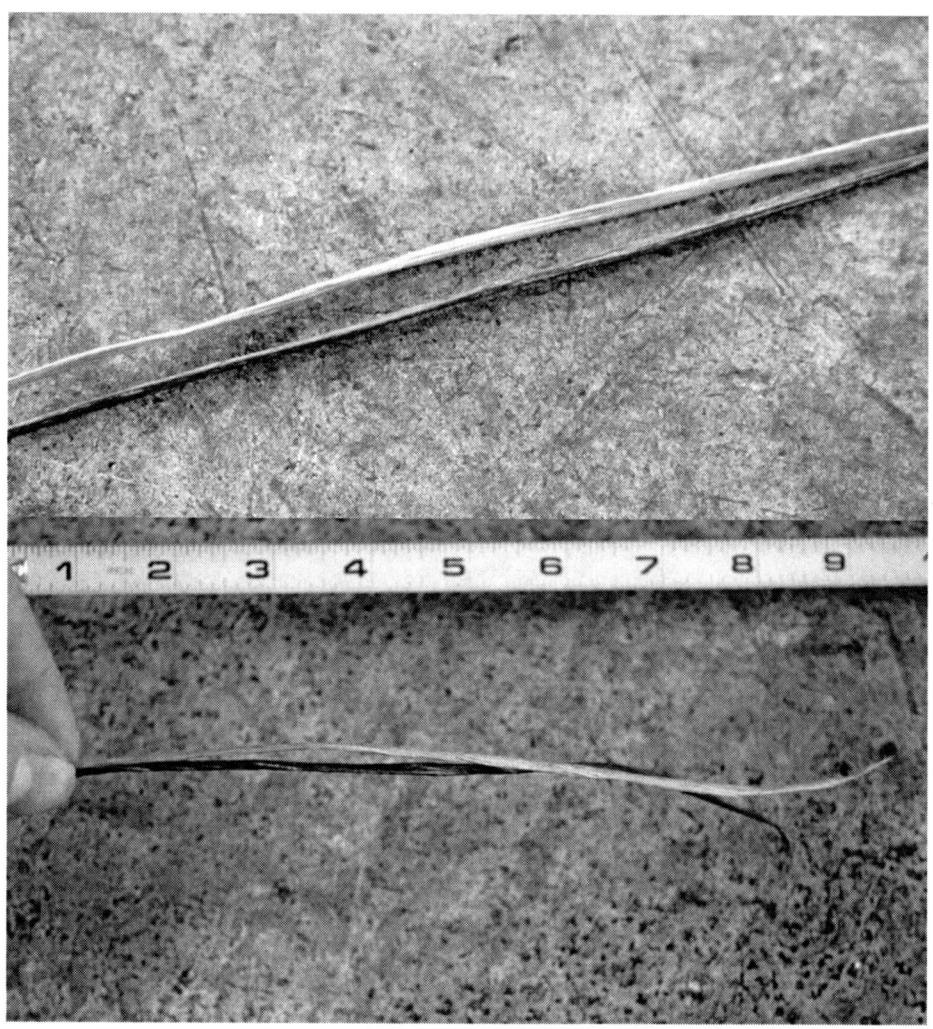

Now that you've got your bundles waxed, grab the ends about eight inches down, next to each other. Now this part is the tricky part that makes the whole thing work. If you know how to counter twist and make rope, then this will be a breeze. If not, it takes a little more doing to get it. If you twist a piece of string in one direction it will start to kink and get harder to twist. Take another string, twist it in the same direction and the same amount of twists, hold them together and let them untwist. They will untwist into each other, inadvertently locking themselves together.

Bonus Track

The Backyard Bowyer

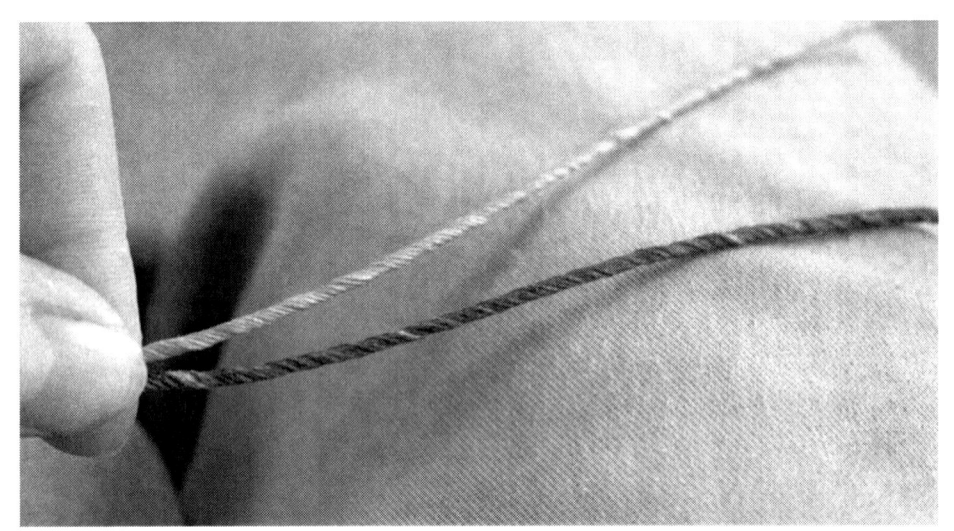

That's the key to this next step. Hold the bundles together at eight inches, then twist each bundle counterclockwise equally, the more the better (but don't go overboard).

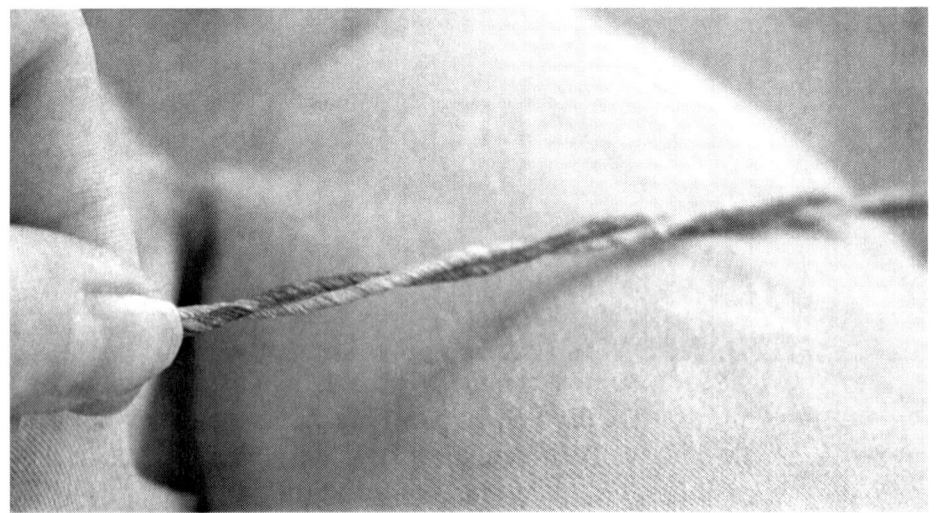

Once they have twisted a good amount, hold them together so that they can untwist into each other, locking the two bundles into one rope.

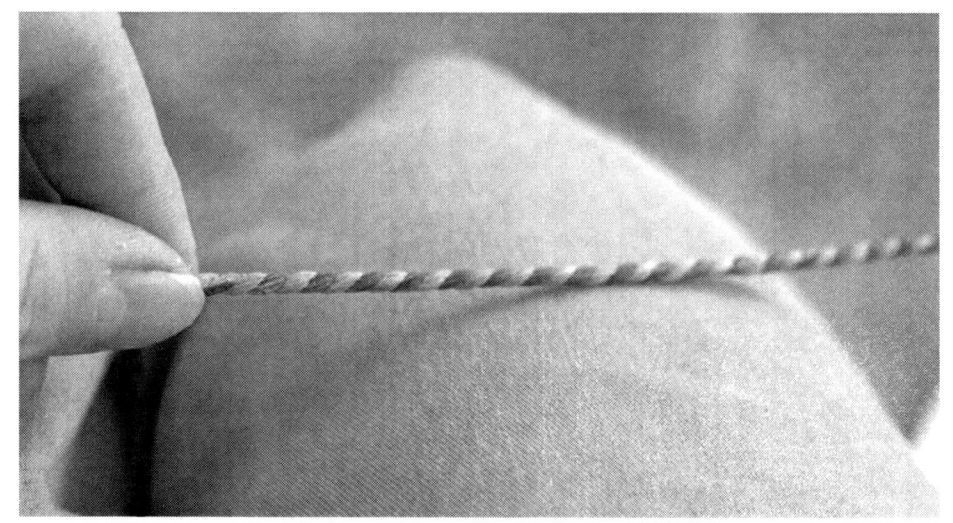

You can twist them a little more just to solidify the connection.

Take the bottom inch and a half of the rope nearest to the rest of the string and fold it over, creating a loop. Either hold this area with your fingers or tie it off.

Bonus Track

The Backyard Bowyer

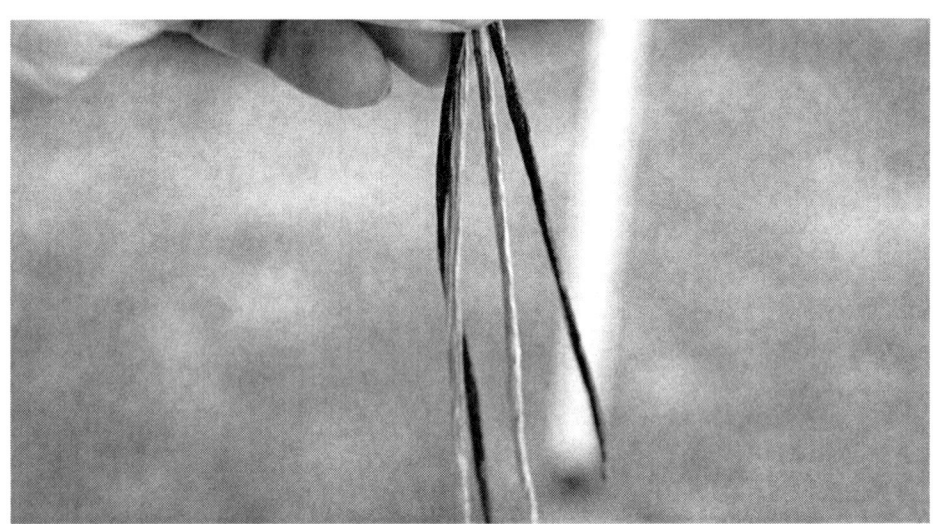

Untwist the shorter end, making sure the loop stays twisted. Now twist that smaller end and the main string bundle clockwise a few times. Now bring one of the short bundles and twist it together with one of the long ones. The clockwise twist will lock them together. Repeat for the other short and long bundle.

Now twist the two newly formed bundles counterclockwise until they begin to kink, then bring them together and let them twist together.

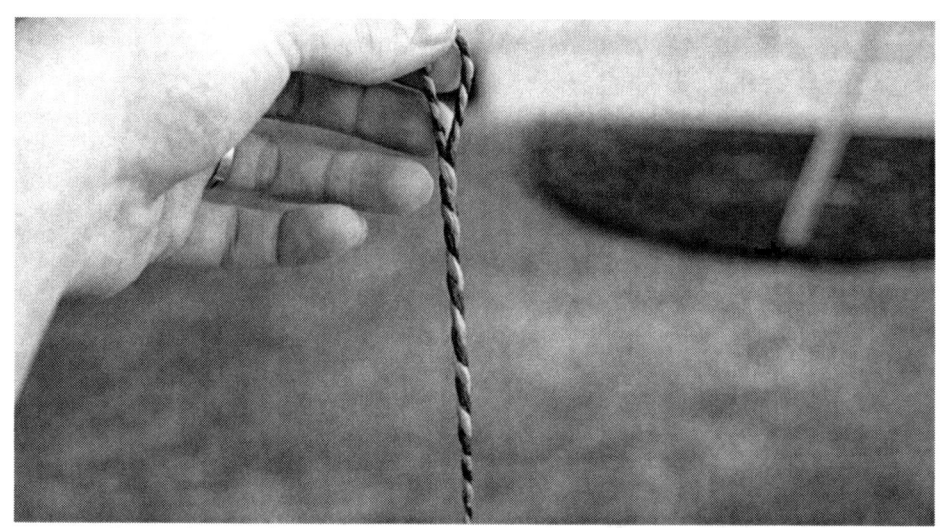

Once they twist together, the loop they form is your top loop.

A little down from the loop, the string will twist in reverse like this. Before going any further, it is important to undo this because it will cause the string to unravel slowly if it isn't taken out. If you plan on putting another loop on the other end of the string, be wary of this happening while you make the second loop.

The Backyard Bowyer

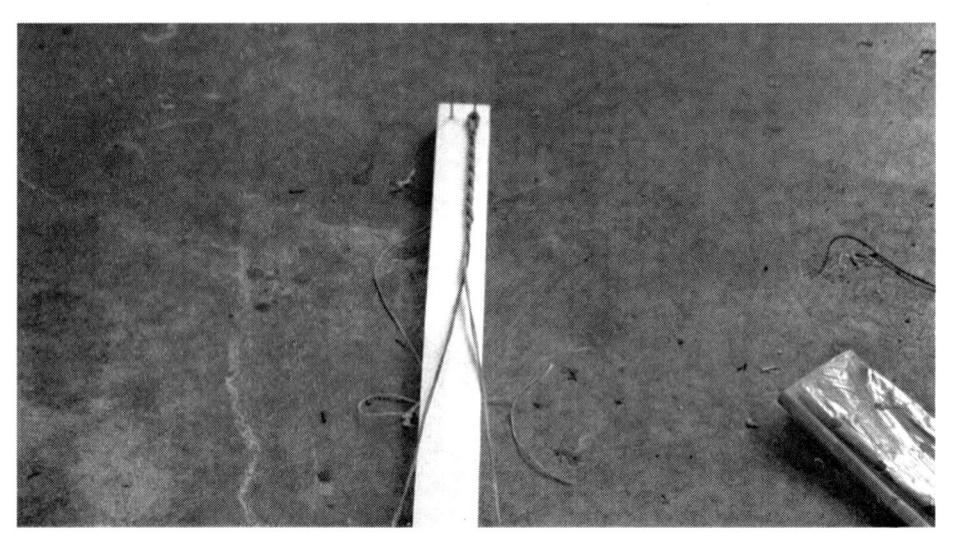

An easy way to take care of that twisting is to anchor the string to a nail or hook and untwist the strands until it is clear like this. Twist the two bundles counterclockwise a little, and let them come together with a very slight twist.

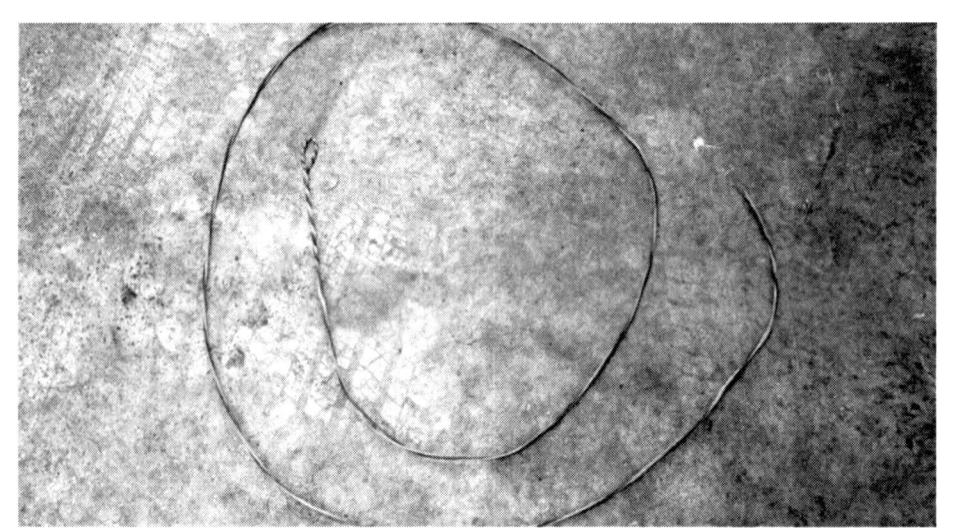

And here is the finished string. For another loop, start off with an extra eight inches and repeat the top loop on the bottom. For a more adjustable string, a timber hitch works very well.

To do a timber hitch, start by grasping where you want your loop to start.

Bring the loose end around the front, making a loop. The loop should be the size of your nock, I'm making it oversized so it is easier to see what I'm doing.

The Backyard Bowyer

Loop the loose end around the back.

Now bring the loose end around the front and then into the loop. Repeat this a couple more times, wrapping the loose end around this inner part of the loop.

And here is the finished knot. Simply place it on the bottom nock, and it will tighten and stay in place. If you need a longer or shorter string, just re-tie it as needed. I really like using this knot for tillering strings and for use on bows that still need a finished string.

The Zombie Slayer Arrow and The Cheater's Dowel Arrow

When it comes to arrows, there are two basic types I make quite often. I do these because they work well and don't break the bank. The Zombie Slayers are the cheaper arrows, what I like to call my disposable arrows. I chose the name because if the zombie apocalypse ever went down and I was stuck in a hardware store, I'd be able to make them in-house, no feathers or fancy parts required. Like most zombie-related items, they are not very consistent, but they are fun for instinctive speed-shooting. They use bamboo or cane plant stakes, duplex nails, and duct tape, things almost any big box hardware store should have for fairly cheap. How cheap? One arrow should cost less than a dollar.

The Cheater's Dowel arrows are my personal favorites for hunting (if hunting, use broadheads instead of field points) and target work. They are about as accurate as wood arrows can be and quite resilient. The reason I call them the Cheater's Dowel arrows is because in most wood

The Backyard Bowyer

arrows, half or more of the price of making one goes into buying shafting. By using hardwood dowels instead of specialty arrow shafting, the only big money spent is on feathers, arrow heads, and nocks. These puppies will probably set you back about $2.50 to three dollars depending on the size and weight of arrow you're going for.

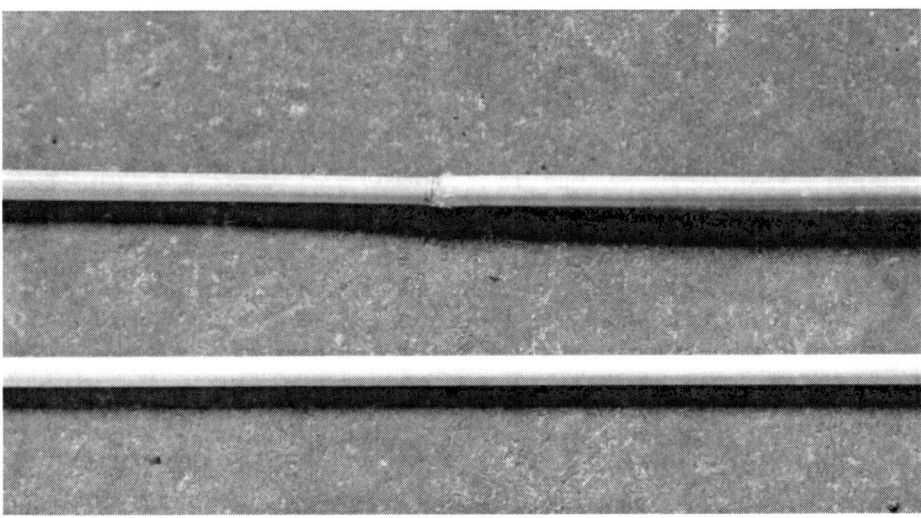

To start, get your material of choice. When selecting bamboo, look for stalks that are not missing chunks, cracking, or have holes in them. Most of the time crooked ones can be straightened, but unless you really want to work for hours, try to find semi-straight stalks. Almost any bamboo or cane will work for these.

With dowels, you want to look for straight grain, just like when building bows. If the dowel is warped, it can be straightened, but if the grain is bad, the arrow could explode, resulting in injury and/or humiliation. Most dowels out there are made of a birch lookalike, though most any hardwood will do. Make sure there are no knots or pieces with both sapwood and heartwood.

With both types of shafts, it is important to pick a diameter that matches your bow's weight. This will get you close to the proper spine, though usually not quite at proper spine. Bamboo is very inconsistent, though dowels are usually pretty safe bets. For bows less than 30 pounds, 1/4 inch diameter shafts work well. From 30 to about 50 pounds, 5/16 inches is a good diameter. For bows from 50 to 65 pounds, 11/32 or 3/8 is the way to go. For anything heavier, 23/64 or 7/16 will do well up to about 80 pounds. Anything heavier should have arrows at least 1/2 an inch, at least near the middle.

Just to make things a little easier, here's a little chart. These are approximate, as spine can vary a great deal. If you have a spine tester or know someone who does (archery shops may let you borrow theirs if they have one) that is the way to go. As a side note, you may not find dowels that match standard archery nocks and points. If that happens, find the next higher diameter dowel, as the point and nock ends can be shaved down and tapered to accommodate the smaller points and nocks.

Bow Weight to Arrow Thickness

Bow Weight	0#-30#	30#-45#	45#-65#	65#-80#	80+#
Standard Shafts	9/32"	5/16"	11/32"	23/64"	1/2"
Dowels	1/4"	5/16"	3/8"	7/16"	1/2"

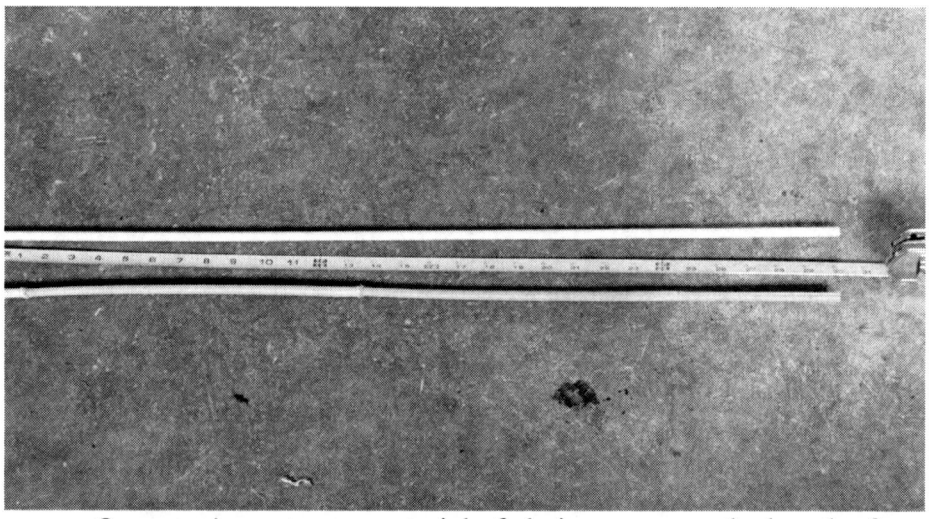

Once you've got your material of choice, measure the length of your arrow, which should be about two inches longer than your draw. Here they are at 30".

Bonus Track

The Backyard Bowyer

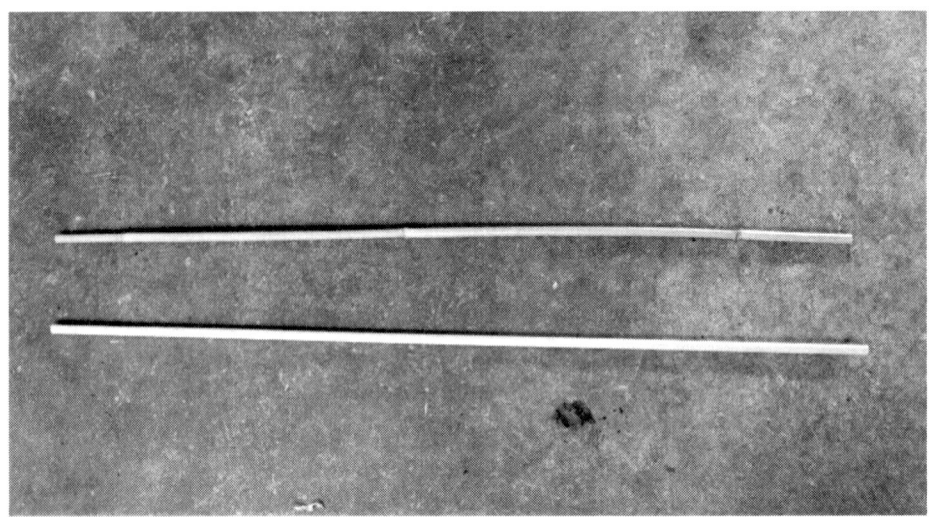

With the two pieces cut out, it is plain to see that neither of them, especially the bamboo one, is straight. There are many ways to straighten an arrow, but my favorite is using dry heat. Dry heat in the form of a propane torch, gas or electric range, or a heat gun will straighten both bamboo and wood shafts. Dry heat has the advantage of not adding moisture like boiling or steaming, but often scorches the wood, though I like the way scorched arrows look.

This is what this crooked piece of bamboo looks like from the end.

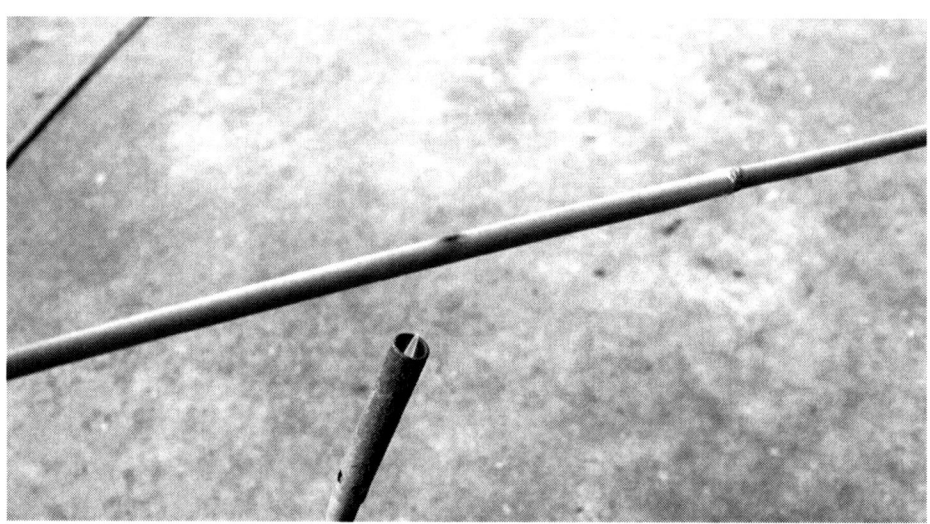

Using your heat source of choice, start at the spots between nodes (the raised bumpy things) and gently heat them up until they become pliable. Once they become pliable, bend them gently in the opposite direction of the warp until the shaft straightens out in that area.

Once the space between nodes is straightened, start working on

The Backyard Bowyer

the nodes themselves. These are the hardest to straighten as most times the way the nodes connect aren't even centered.

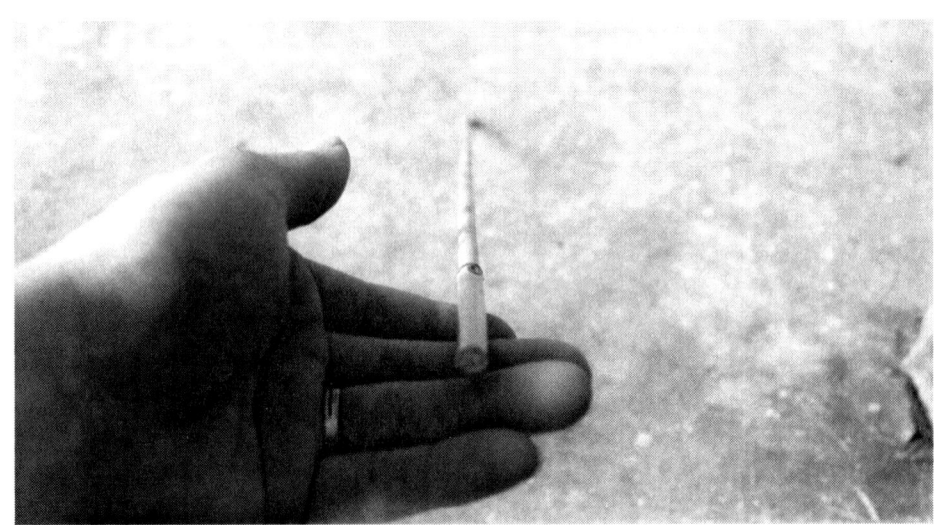

Once the straightening is done, I like to heat the whole shaft up and give it a nice striped scorched look.

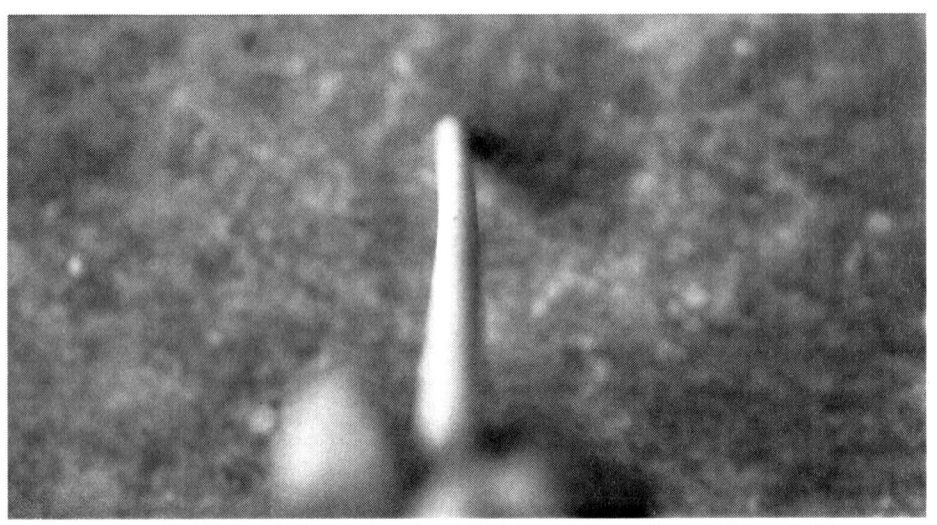

Now we'll straighten the dowel. It may have looked straight before, but looking down the end will let you know if it's straight or not.

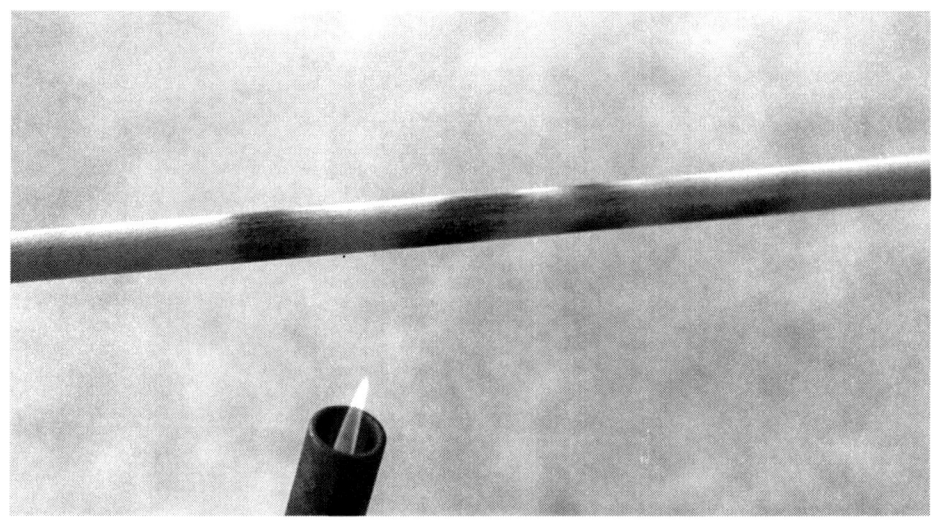

Just like the bamboo shaft, heat the warped spots until the wood gets pliable. With actual wood, be very careful to keep the heat low and far from the surface, as it can burn very easily. Once straightened, I usually scorch the whole shaft. If done slowly, this also can help keep the arrow from losing its stiffness and straightness over time.

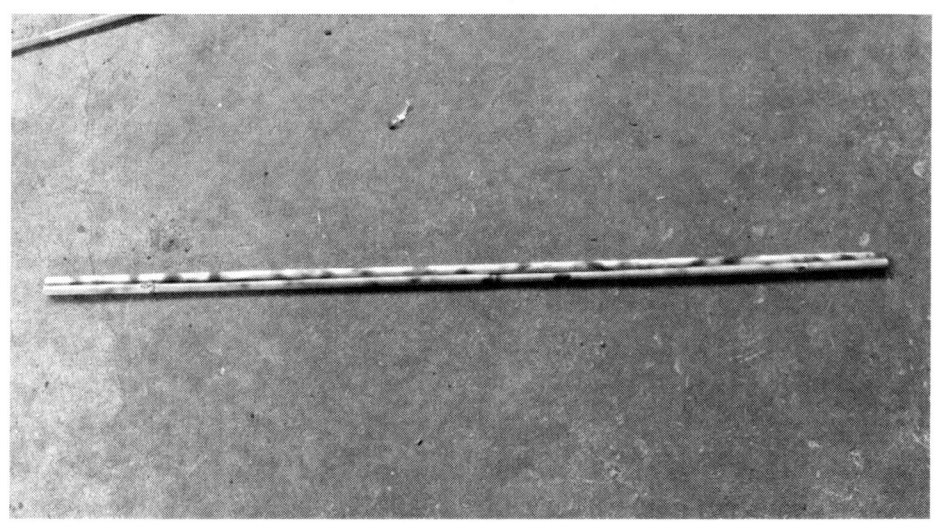

Here are our arrow shafts ready for nocks, points, and fletching.

The Backyard Bowyer

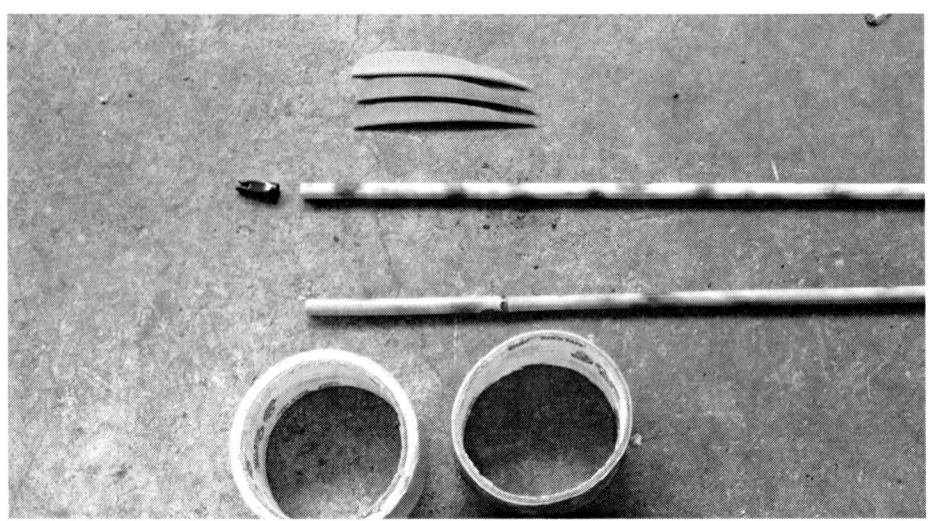

    For fletching and nocking the Cheater's Dowel arrow, you need three ground and trimmed feathers in your choice of shape, color, and length, and a glue-on nock. For the Zombie Slayer, all you need is some duct tape. Two different colors gives a nice effect.

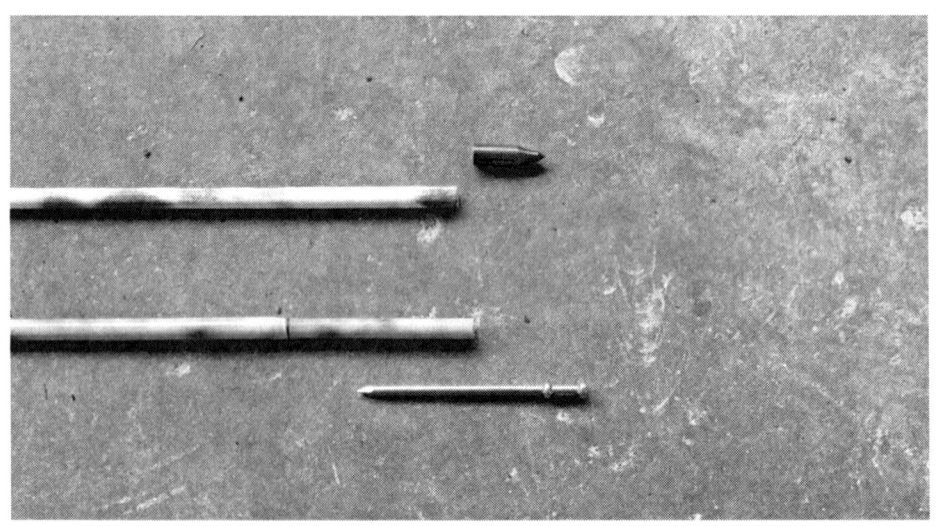

    As for points, the Cheater's Dowel uses a glue-on field point, or any glue-on point of choice, and the Zombie slayer uses a 16D duplex nail.

172

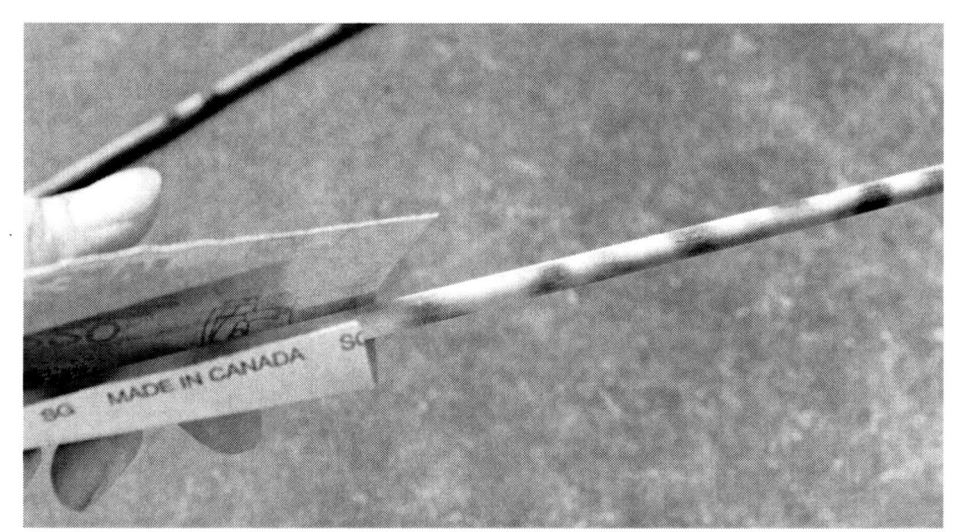

We'll start with the dowel arrow. Just to clean it up a little and make it smooth, sand it lightly with 220 or higher grit paper. A finish can also he applied to the shaft now.

In order for the nock and point to fit, the shaft needs to be tapered. The easiest way to taper the shaft is to use a manual pencil sharpener like this one. This way, only a little bit of adjusting is needed, rather than shaping the taper by hand.

The Backyard Bowyer

For the nock end, The taper itself can be left alone. Most glue on nocks require a flat tip, not a point, in order to fit properly.

If this is the case, as it is with mine, simply file off the tip of the tapered end and test-fit it.

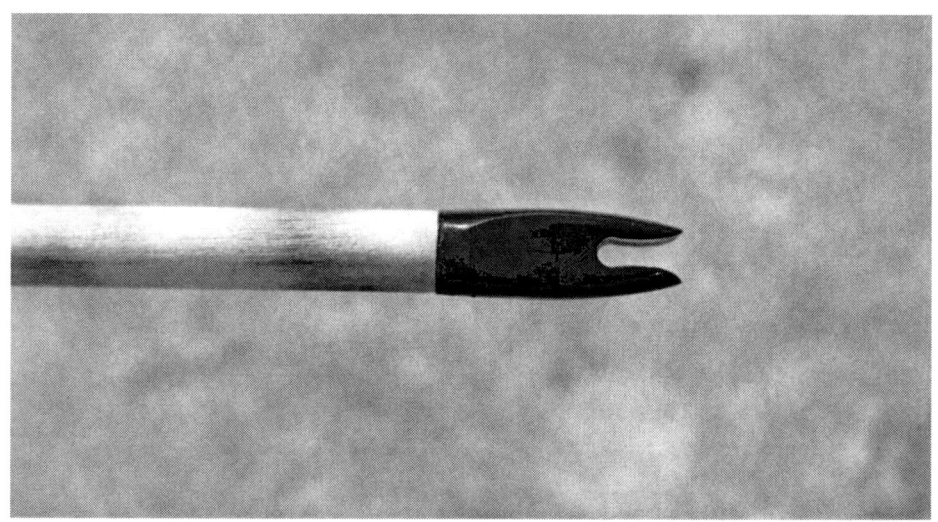

Once the nock fits, glue it into place with super glue, waterproof wood glue, or hot melt glue. Some nocks fit flush to the shaft, though if you are using a dowel that does not match standard nocks and tips, there may be some exposed taper behind the nock.

The point usually needs more of a taper, so simply file the taper near the base until the point fits.

The Backyard Bowyer

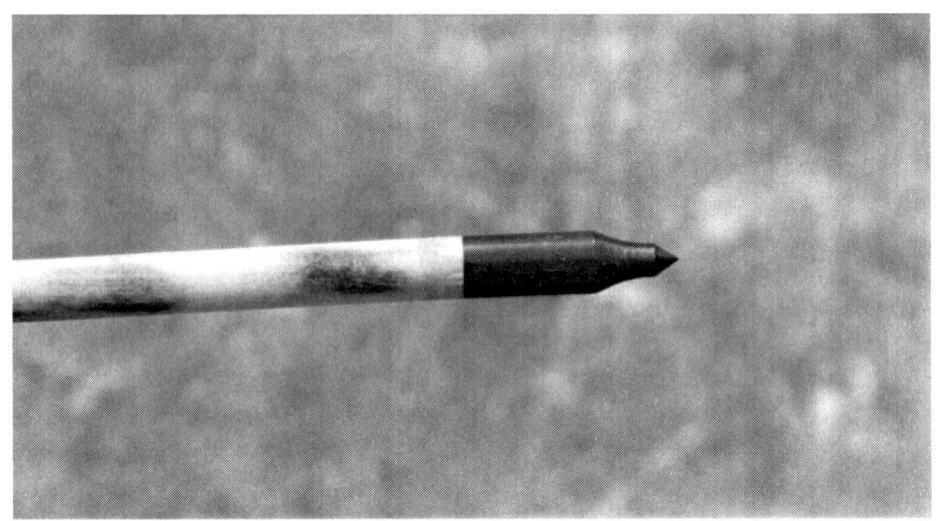

Once the point fits, glue it in place.

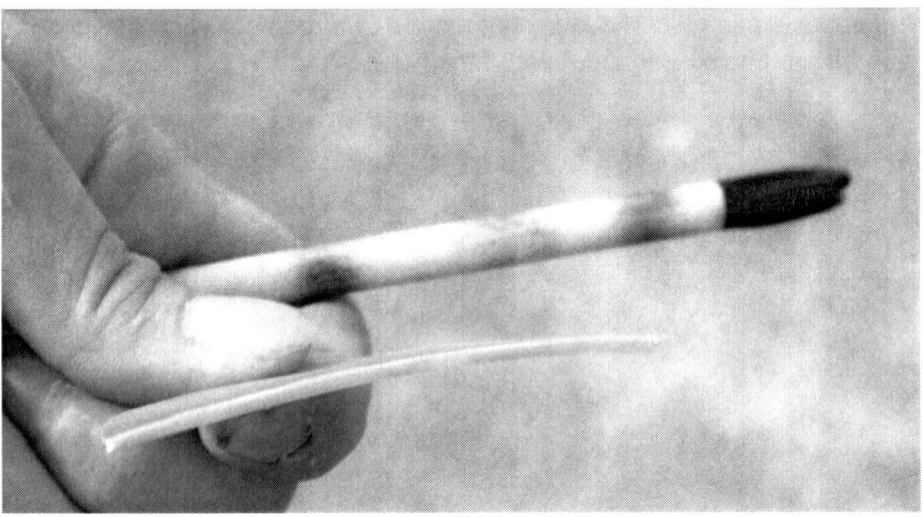

Using super glue or any other instant glue, glue the feathers to the shaft. There are fletching jigs available, but I do all my fletching by hand. I usually start my fletching an inch down from the bottom of the string grove on the nock. Make sure the feather's ribs are all facing the nock end of the arrow, so that they lay down smoothly when fired.

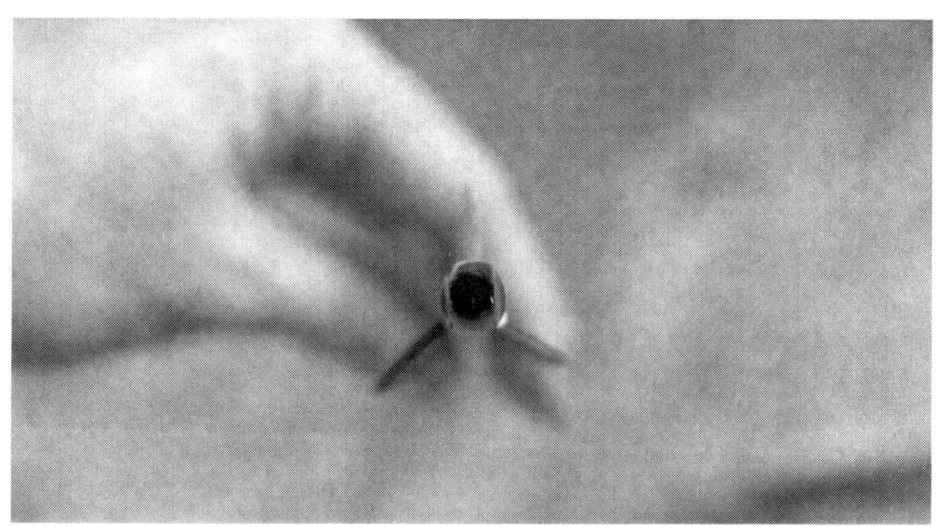

Follow this pattern as best you can, if fletching by hand. The odd feather is glued on perpendicular to the string groove in the nock. The other two feathers are glued on separating the arrow into three equal slices.

The front ends of the feathers are usually sharp and stick out a bit, so a little sanding keeps them from cutting you or getting stuck in your hand when shooting.

The Backyard Bowyer

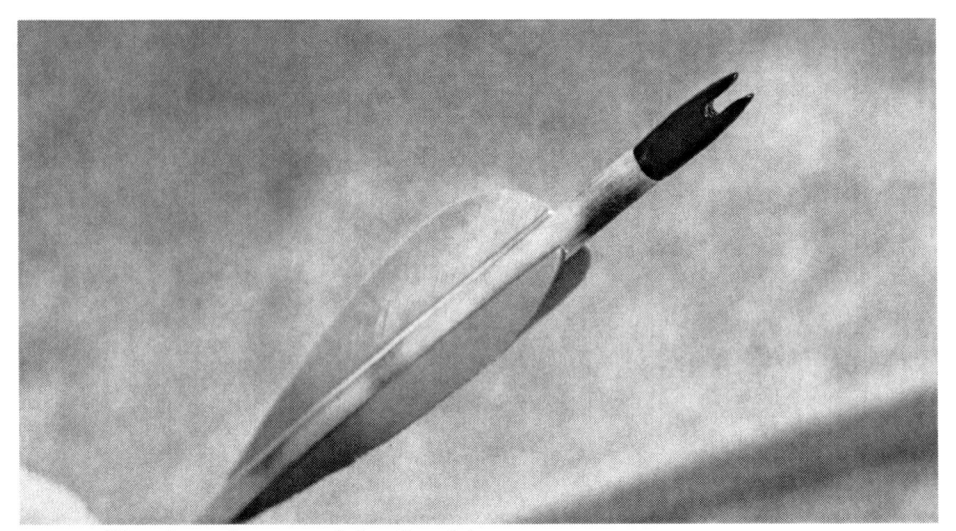

Here's a closeup of the fletching.

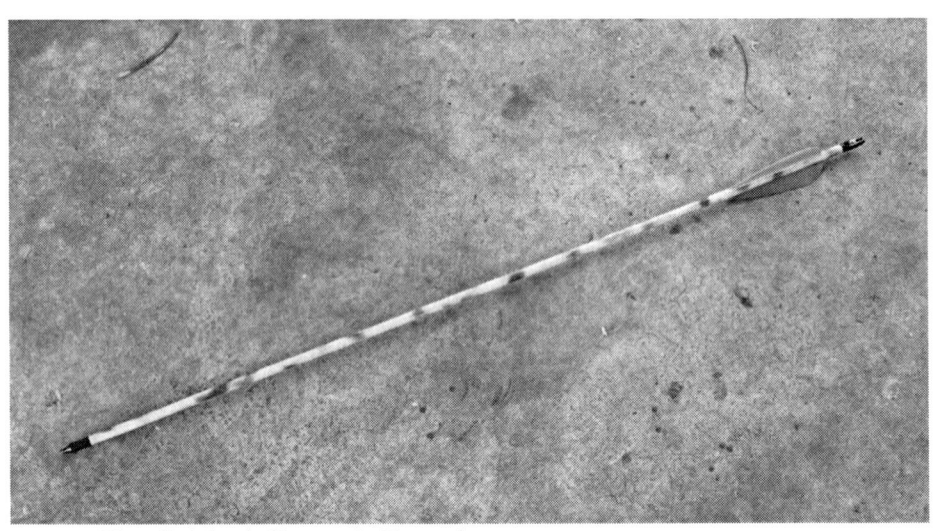

The finished Cheater's Dowel arrow.

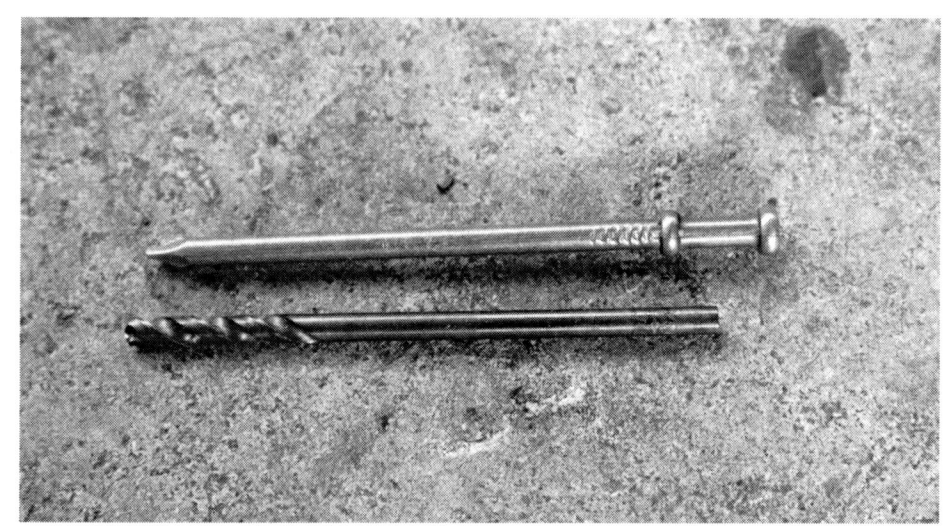

The first step to assembling the Zombie Slayer is to find a drill bit the same diameter as the duplex nail. This type of tip works well with bamboo and cane because they already have centered holes that the drill bit will follow.

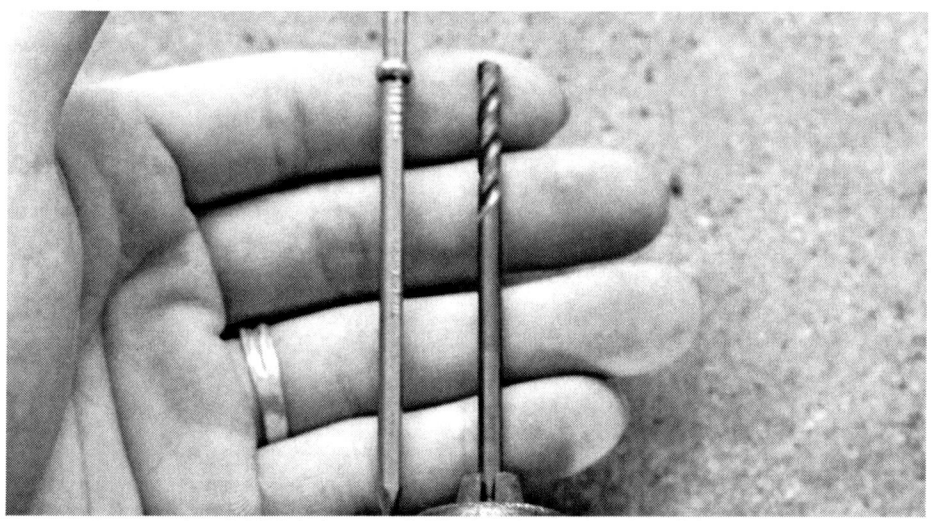

Insert the drill bit into a drill chuck so that it will go as deep as the nail's shank will go like in the picture.

Bonus Track 179

The Backyard Bowyer

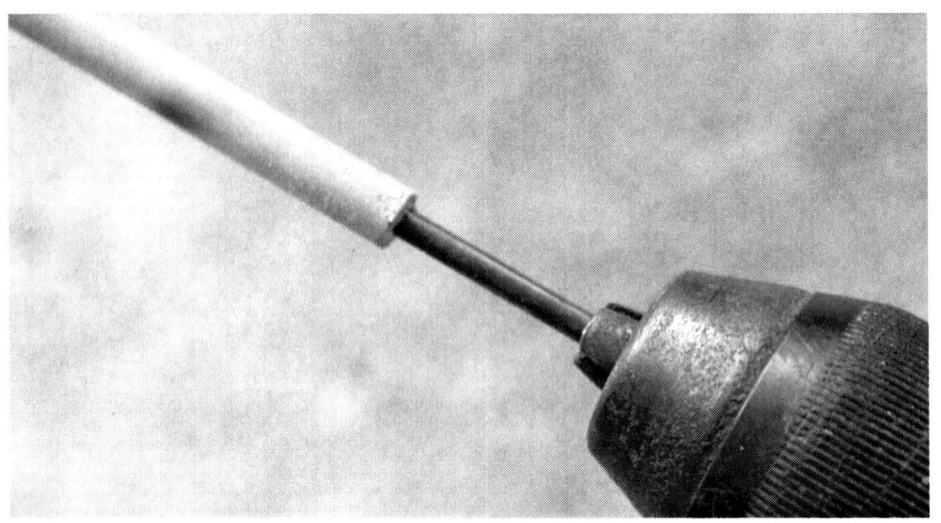

Working slowly, drill into the front end of the bamboo shaft, following the natural hollow in the bamboo. Drilling too quickly may split the shaft at this point.

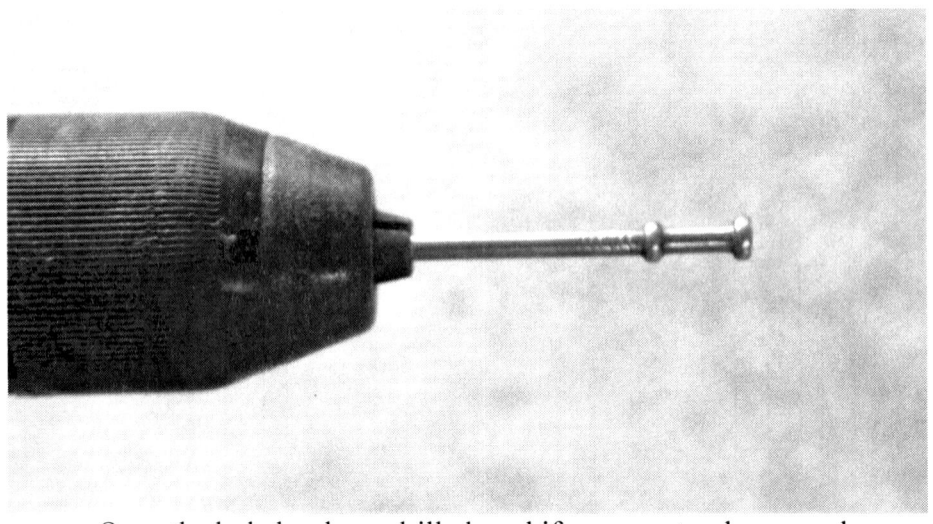

Once the hole has been drilled, and if you want a sharp, nock field-point, chuck the duplex nail into the drill. If not, the arrow will be slightly blunt, though much faster to produce.

180

With a file, run the drill while filing the point of the nail. This will ensure that the point is centered. A powered sander or grinder can really help speed things up, but this can be done with just a file and the drill. It takes much longer, but this can also be done with just a file, without the drill.

Once the point is ground, test-fit the nail. It should go in smoothly until the little ridges near the first nail head.

The Backyard Bowyer

Glue the nail in place. You may need to tap it lightly with a hammer to get it to be fully seated. If for than a little force is required, be sure to hold the arrow straight while tapping with the hammer because holding it at an angle could possibly break the shaft.

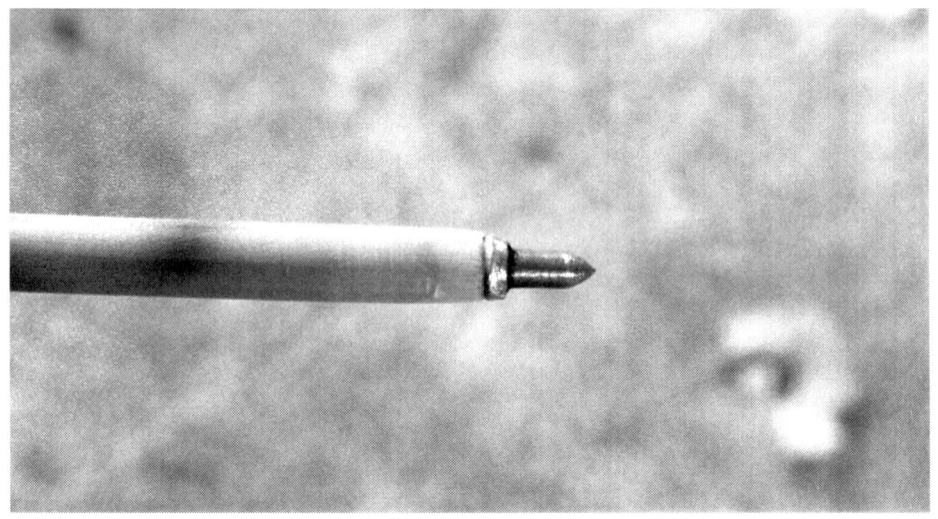

Once the glue has dried, use a file and sandpaper to bring the bamboo down to the level of the nail's head. This makes the point harder to break. For quicker arrows, the nails don't need to be sharpened. They still work on most soft or foam targets.

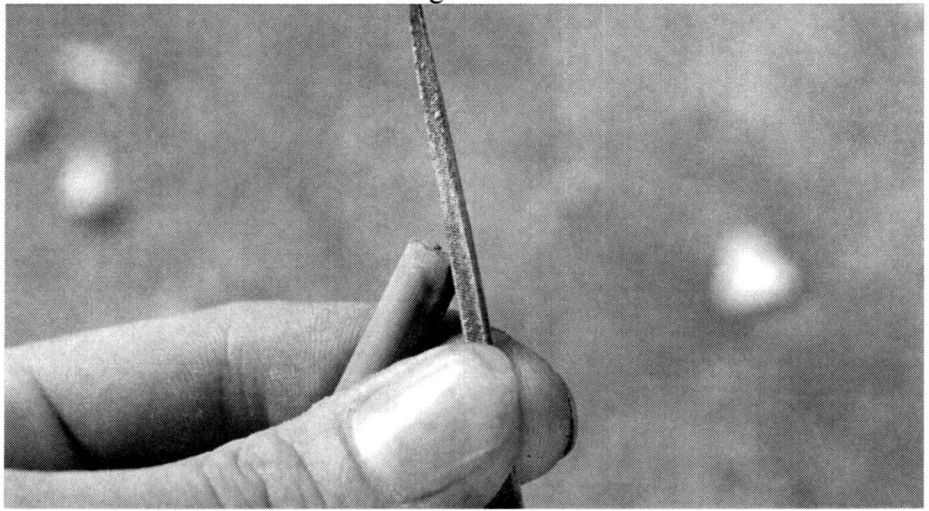

On the nock end, use a file to start the string groove. This first cut should be about one eighth of an inch wide and just as deep.

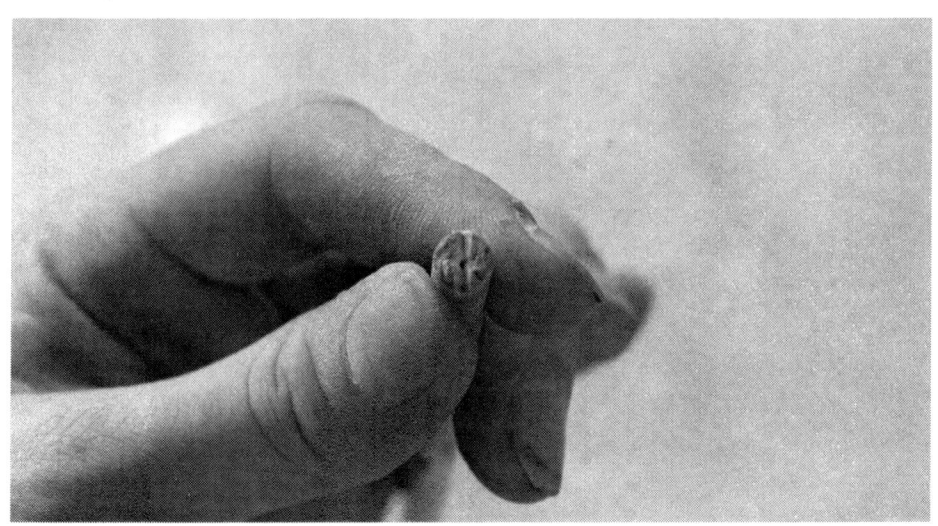

Here is the beginning of the groove. What we are doing is creating what is called a self nock, meaning the nocking point is built into the shaft. This first file groove will help guide us as we cut the rest of the nock.

The Backyard Bowyer

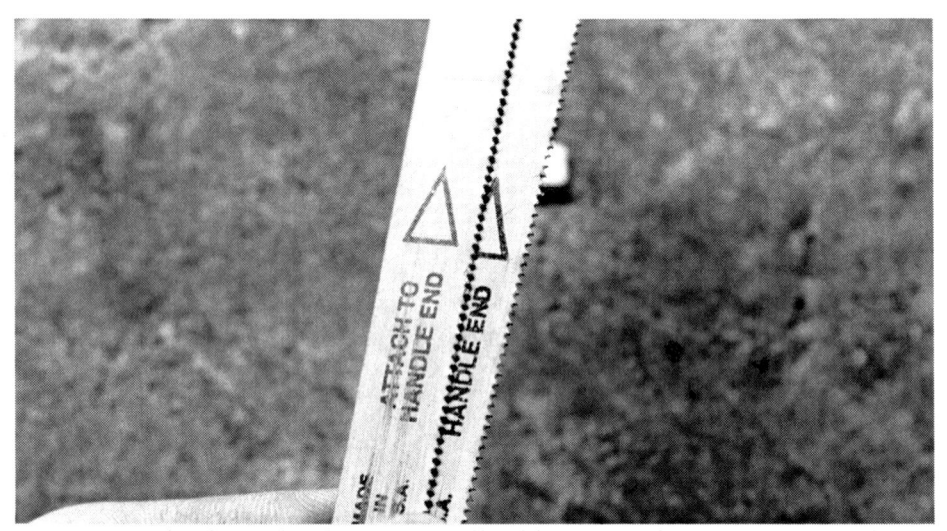

Two hacksaw blades are usually thick enough to create a good-sized nock. To find out if it will work, measure the saw blades against your string to determine how many blades you need.

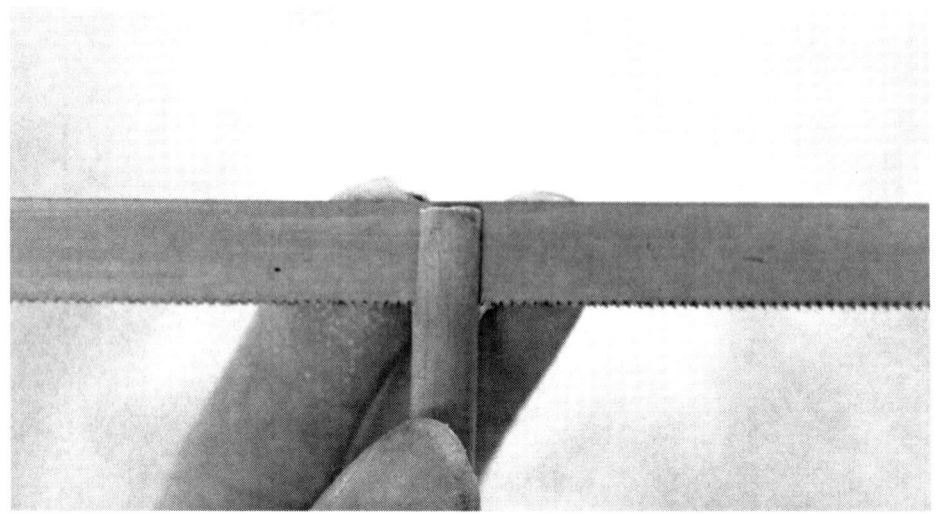

Tape the blades together and cut down into the shaft. Try to go as straight as possible, down to about the depth of the saw's cut.

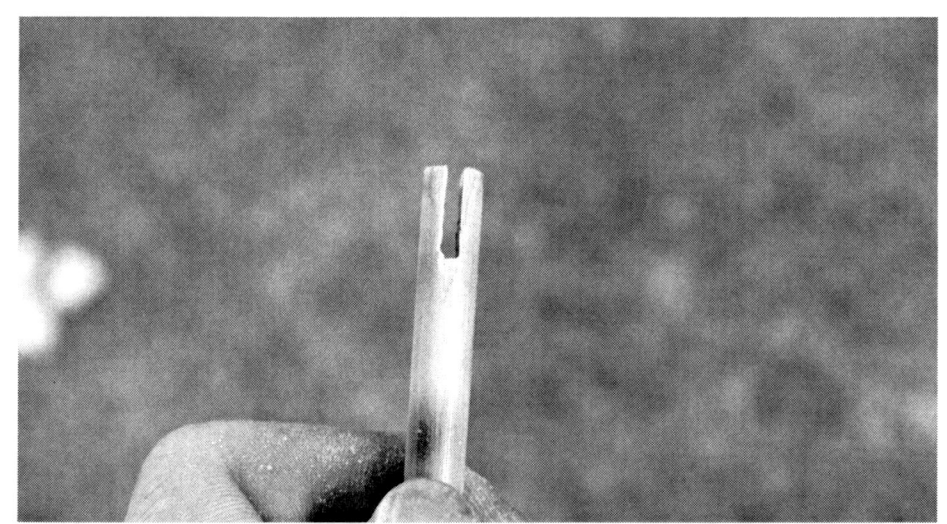

The nock should look like this. If the groove is big enough, this is all you need, though if the groove is a little tight, we can add a bottom to this nock which will allow it to grip the string much like a plastic nock.

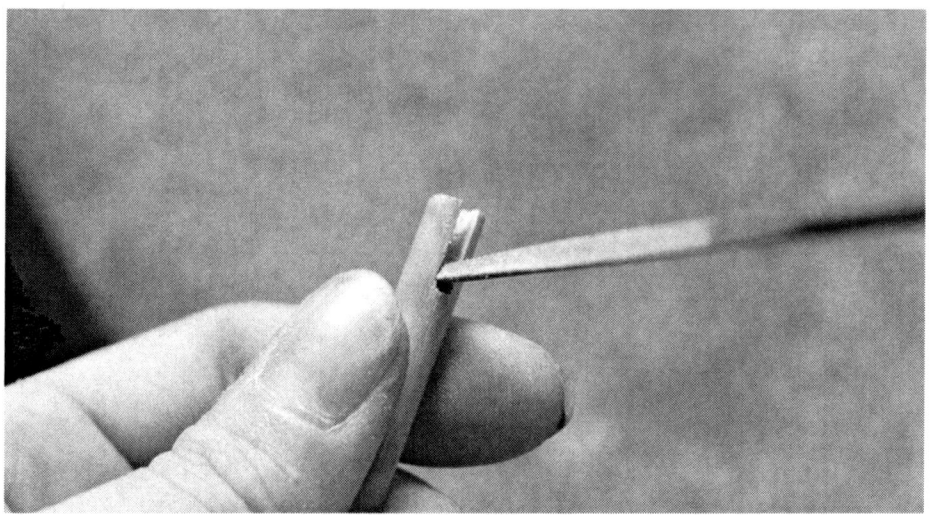

Starting with a triangular file, twist it in the base of the nock on both sides until it is large enough to accept the rat tail file. It is a good idea to get a set of rat tail files that match different string thicknesses.

Bonus Track

The Backyard Bowyer

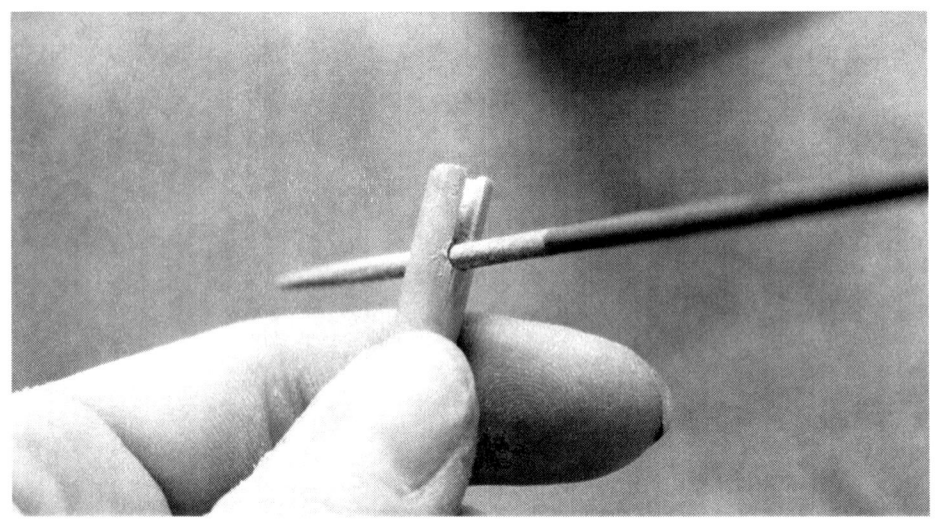

Once the rat tail file fits, use it to open the bottom up a little, and clean up the bottom of the nock.

This is what the nock should now look like.

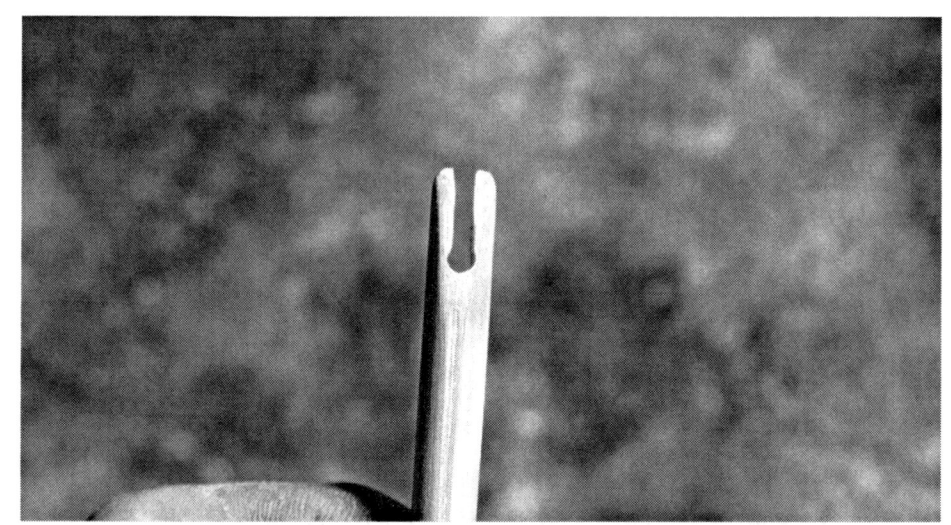

To make the arrow more comfortable to hold and put less strain on the rest of the arrow shaft, file or sand the nock down to a flat, similar to a glue-on nock.

Here's what the nock should look like from the side.

The Backyard Bowyer

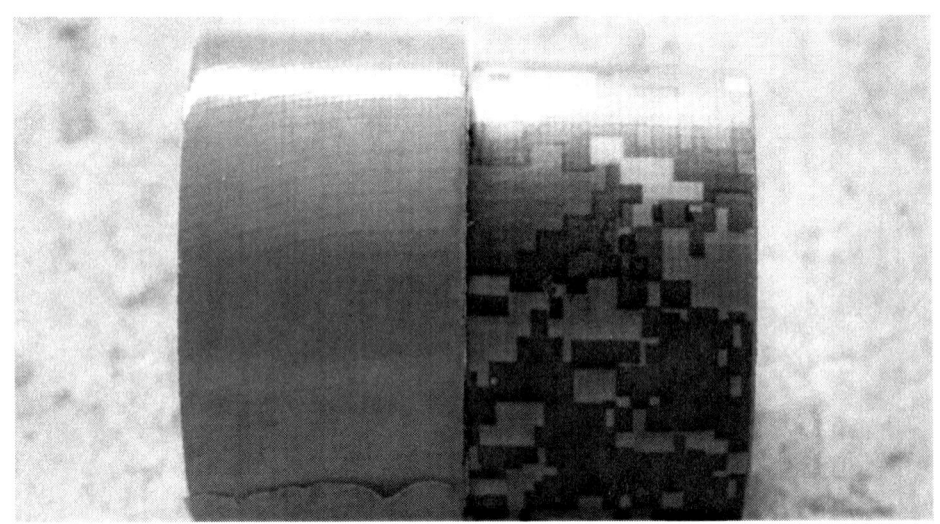

To fletch the Zombie Slayer, we'll be using duct tape, or what I like to call Miracle Fletch. Duct tape is great because it is self-adhesive, somewhat waterproof, and makes a fairly accurate fletching. Its downside is that like plastic arrow vanes, duct tape will cause the arrow to kick off of the bow and arrow rest when fired, though for quick and cheap it can't be beat.

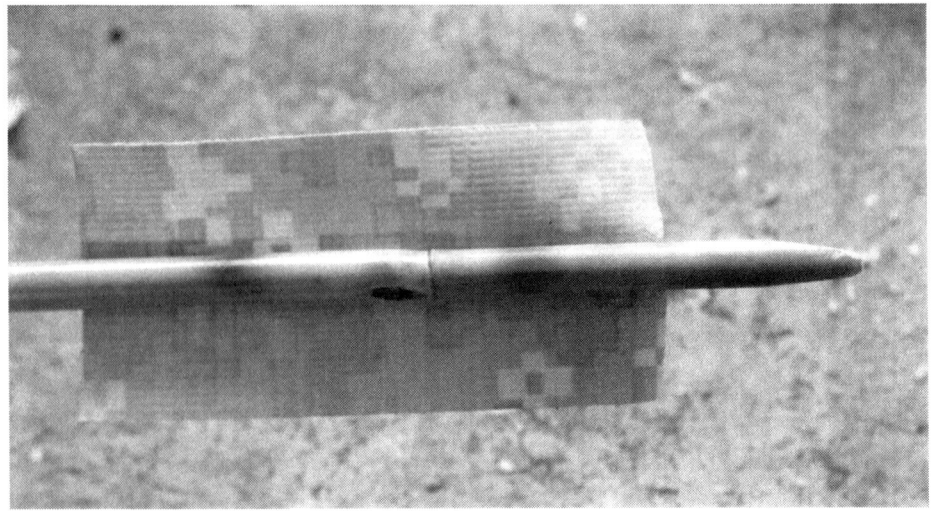

Place a four inch strip of duct tape (longer if your want longer fletchings, shorter if you want shorter fletchings) on one side of the shaft, about an inch down from the bottom of the nock's groove. Try to center it as much as possible.

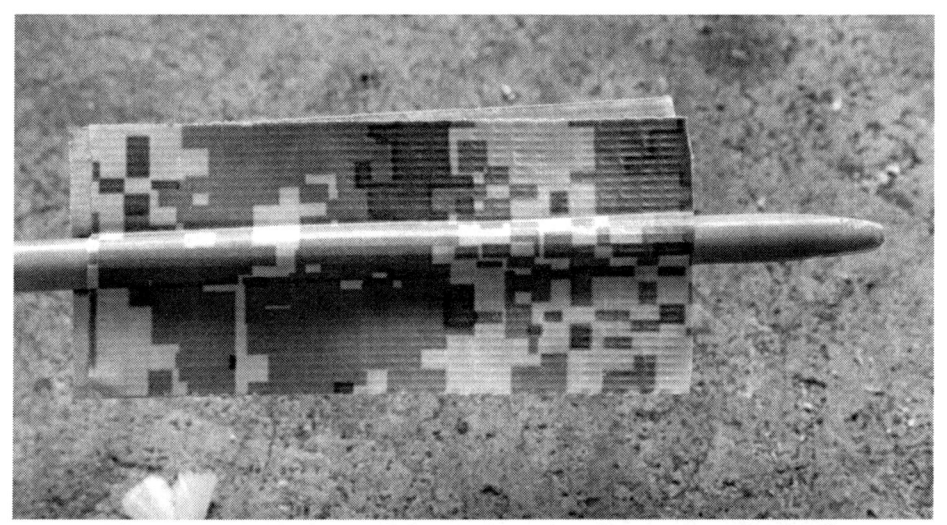

Place a second piece of the same color duct tape over the first, then press them together so that they stick like this.

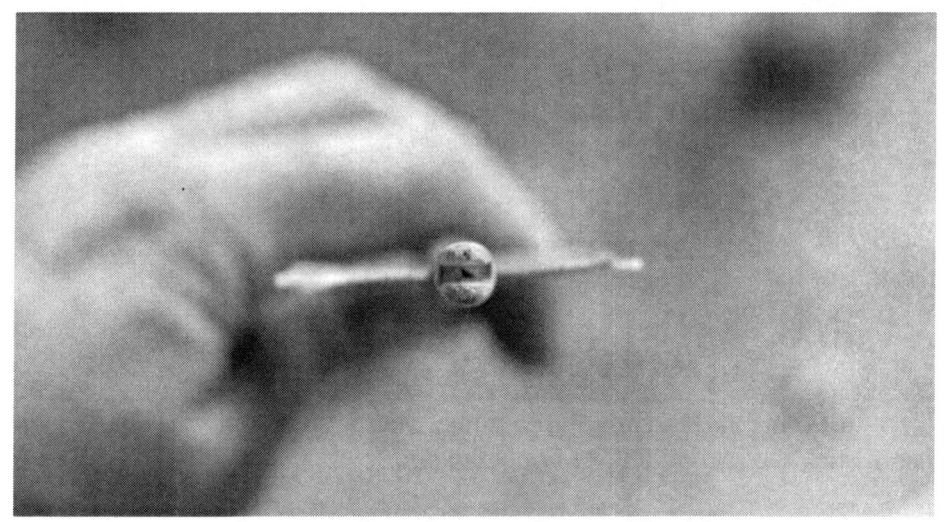

You want the two strips of tape to line up like this.

The Backyard Bowyer

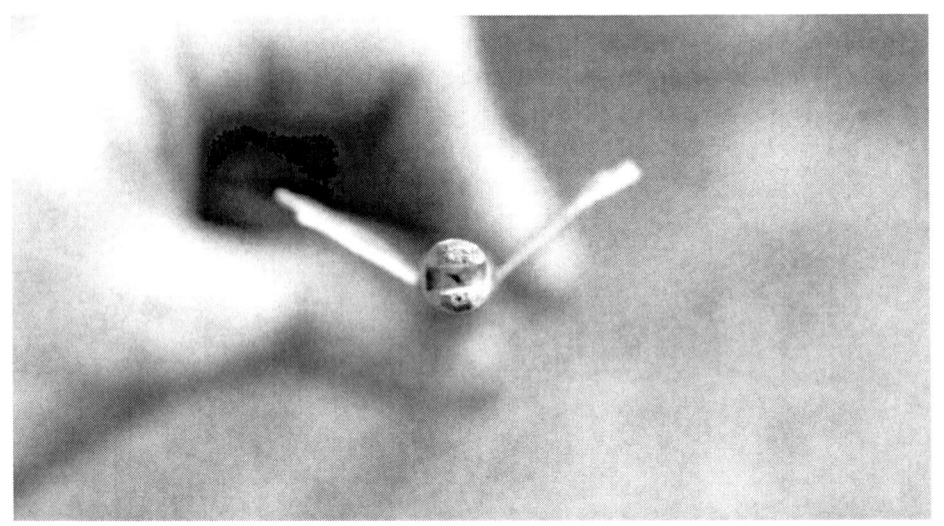

Since we are going for the standard three-vane fletch, fold the two vanes to one side.

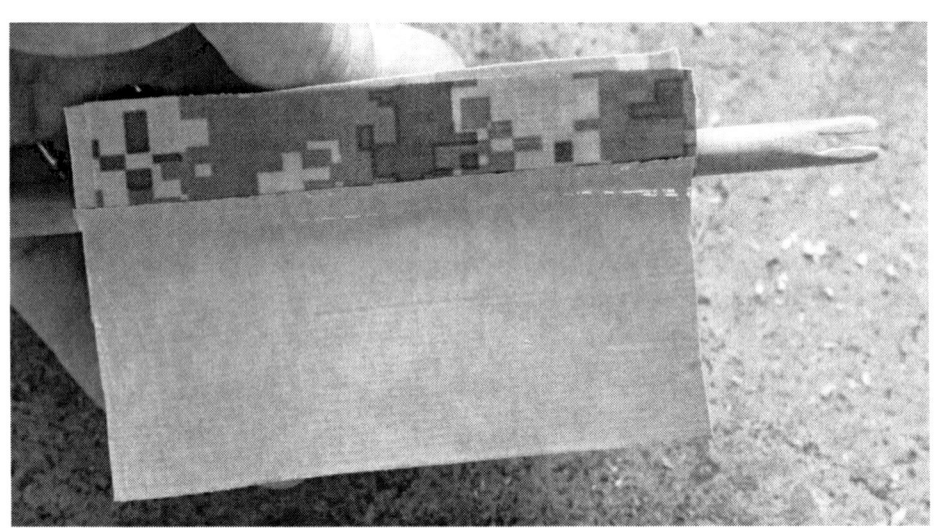

Starting at the seam of one fletch where it runs onto the shaft itself, stick the second color of duct tape on.

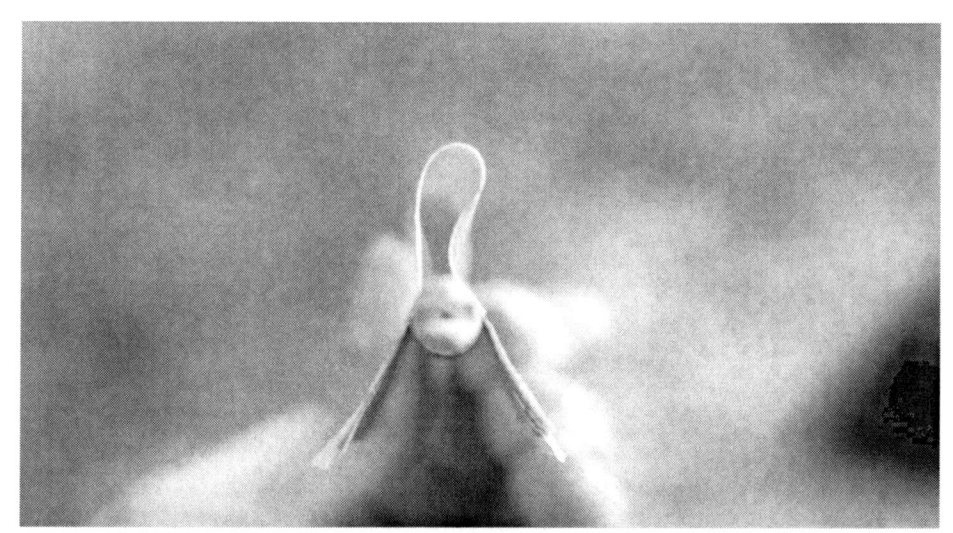

Fold the strip of tape over and stick it to the seam on the other side. It should look like this from the end.

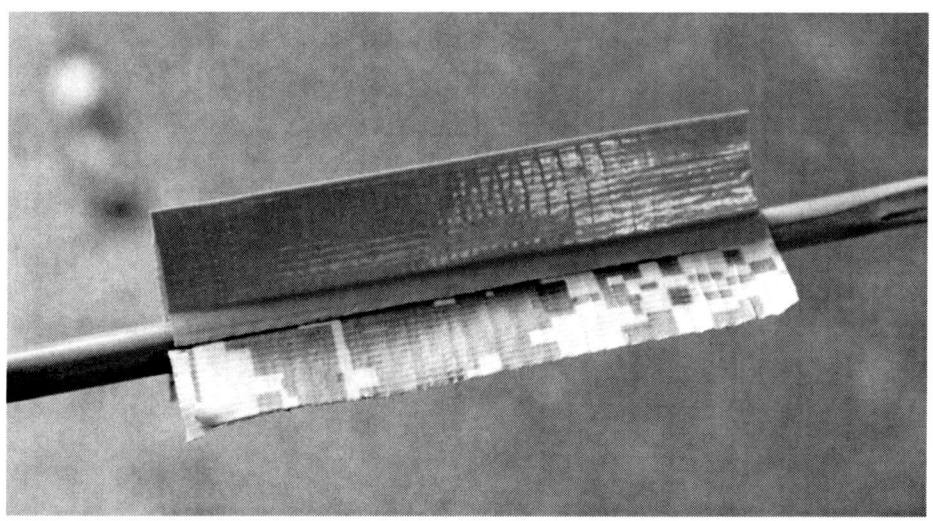

Press the two sides together and flatten the vane just like the other two.

The Backyard Bowyer

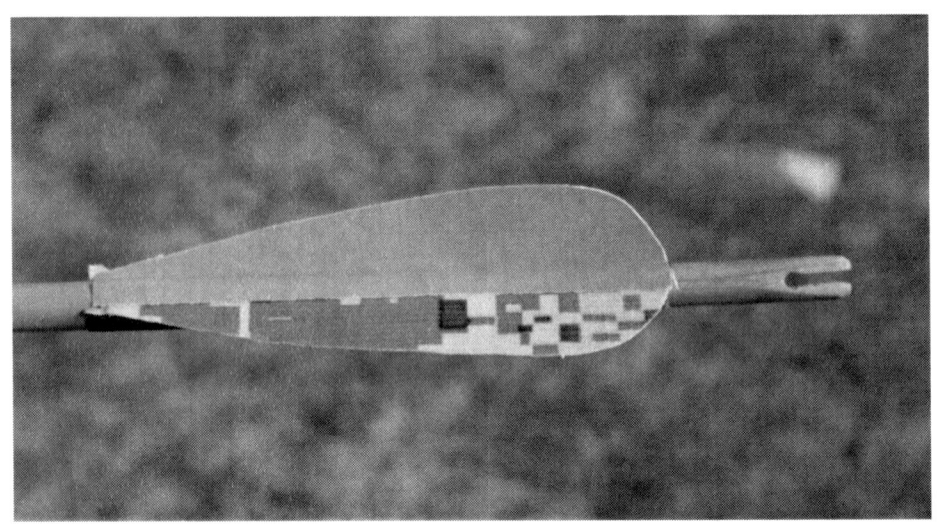

With a knife or pair of scissors, cut the shape of your choice out of the duct tape, creating your vanes. Here is one type of shape that I often use, which is the same shape as the feathers I buy.

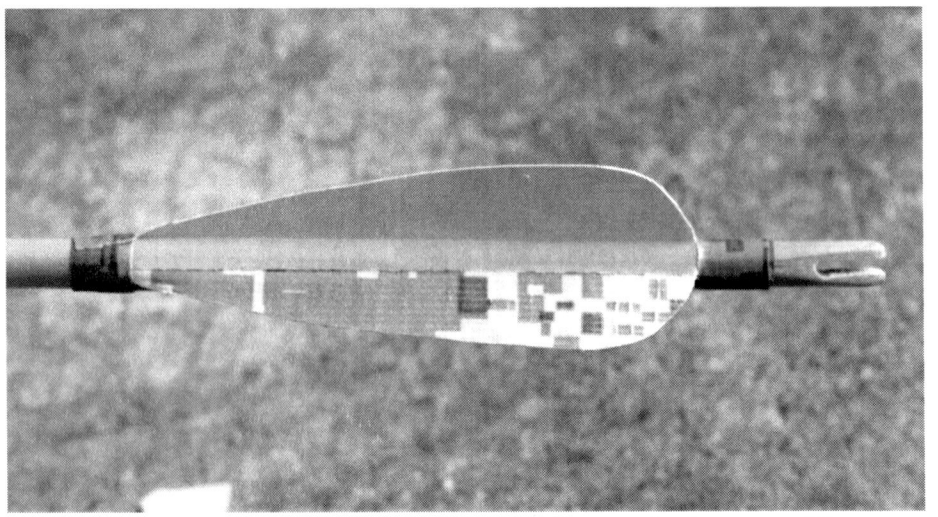

Take two small strips of duct tape and wrap the bottom of the fletchings to keep them from ripping off with use, and the top of the fletchings near the nock to help keep the nock from splitting.

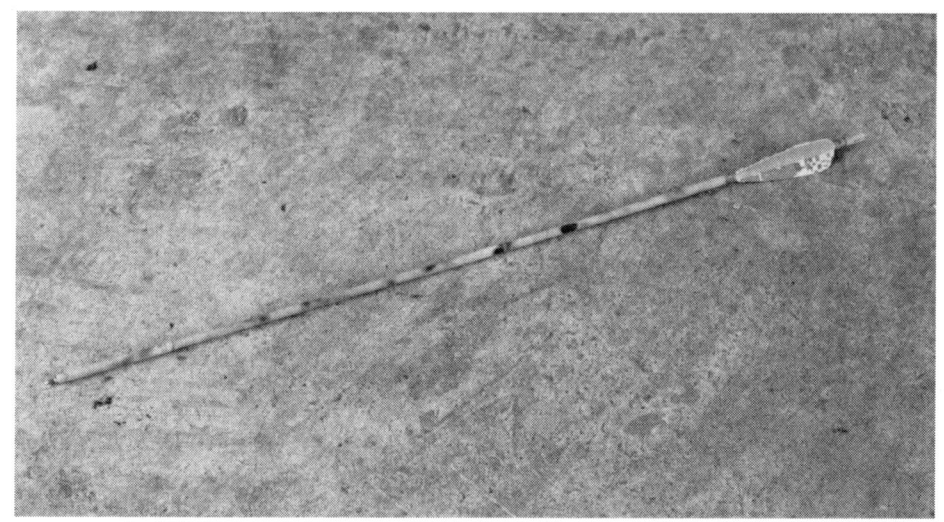

Here it is, the Zombie Slayer in all its glory.

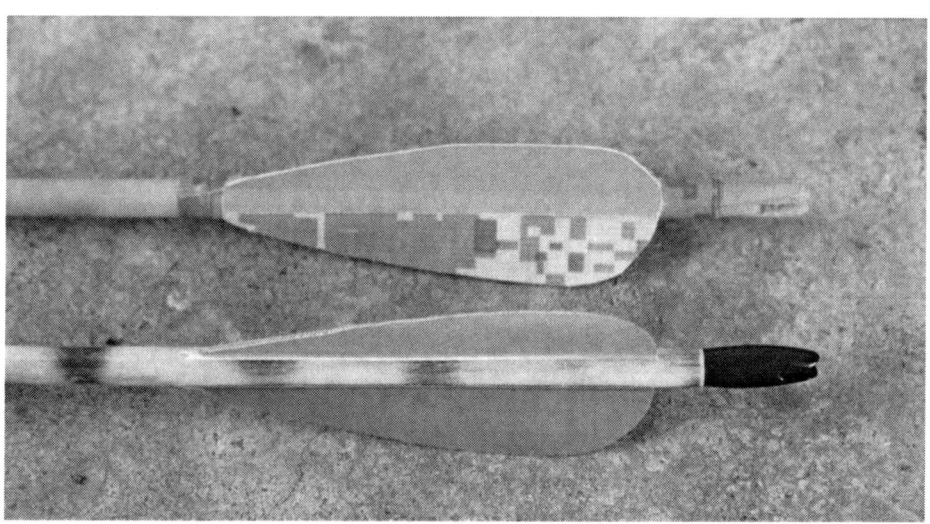

Here are the two arrows at the nock ends. Remember, everything is interchangeable. You can do self nocks with dowels, just don't forget to wrap it with tape or strong thread. Glue on nocks also work on bamboo, and the fletchings go on the same for either shaft material.

Bonus Track 193

The Backyard Bowyer

Looking at the tips, you can see how the duplex nail mimics the glue-on field point. Nails can be used for dowels, but drilling the hole may be difficult. Cutting the nail down to half an inch or an inch may help.

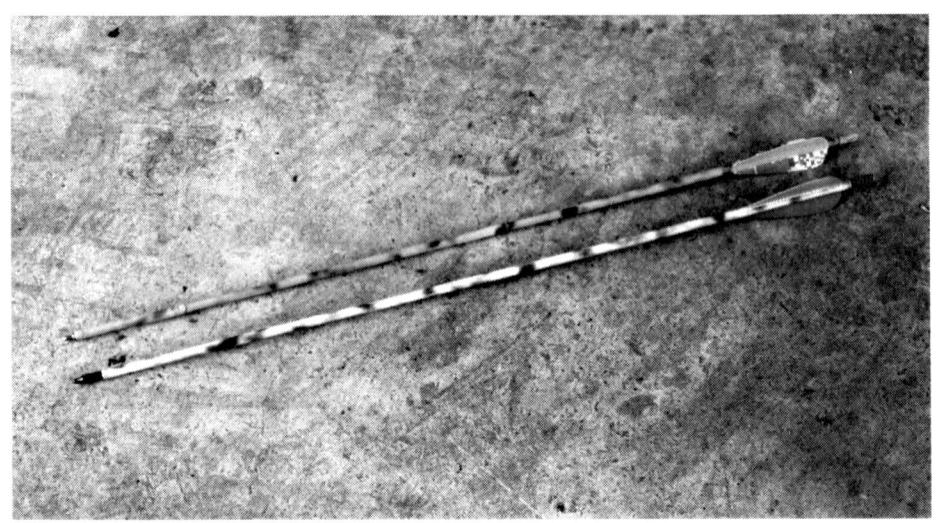

Now that you've got your arrows, you can get shooting! That's it for the bonus track, if you want more bow stuff, go back to page one, that's what I'd do.

194